Programmed Learning Aid for
INTERMEDIATE ACCOUNTING
Volume 1

Programmed Learning Aid for

INTERMEDIATE ACCOUNTING

VOLUME 1

GLENN A. WELSCH, Ph.D.
The John Arch White Professor of Accounting
The University of Texas at Austin
and Certified Public Accountant (CPA)

WALTER T. HARRISON, JR., Ph.D.
Assistant Professor of Accounting
The University of Texas at Austin
and Certified Public Accountant (CPA)

Coordinating Editor
ROGER H. HERMANSON
Georgia State University

LEARNING SYSTEMS COMPANY

 A division of
RICHARD D. IRWIN, INC.   Homewood, Illinois   60430

Also available through
IRWIN-DORSEY LIMITED   Georgetown, Ontario   L7G 4B3

ISBN 0-256-02005-1
Printed in the United States of America

1 2 3 4 5 6 7 8 9 0 K 6 5 4 3 2 1 0 9 8 7

FOREWORD

Each of the books constituting the Programmed Learning Aid Series is in programmed learning format to provide the reader with a quick, efficient, and effective means of grasping the essential subject matter.

The specific benefits of the programmed method of presentation are as follows:

1. It keeps the reader *active* in the learning process and increases comprehension level.
2. Incorrect responses are *corrected immediately*.
3. Correct responses are *reinforced immediately*.
4. The method is *flexible*. Those who need more "tutoring" receive it because they are encouraged to reread frames in which they have missed any of the questions asked.
5. The method makes learning seem like a game.

The method of programming used in this PLAID on intermediate accounting and in most of the other PLAIDs is unique and simple to use. Begin by reading Frame 1[1] in Chapter 1. At the end of that frame answer the True-False questions given. To determine the correctness of your responses, merely turn the page and examine the answers given in Answer frame 1[1]. You are told *why* each statement is true or false. Performance on the questions given is used as a measure of your understanding of all the materials in Frame 1[1]. If any of the questions are missed, reread Frame 1[1] before continuing on to Frame 2[1]. This same procedure should be used throughout the book. Specific instructions are given throughout as to where to turn next to continue working the program.

You may desire to go through the PLAID a second time leaving out the programmed questions and answers, or to test your understanding by going through it a second time, answering all of the questions once again and rereading only those frames in which comprehension is unsatisfactory.

PLAIDs are continuously updated in new printings to provide readers with the latest subject content in the field.

Dr. Welsch, coauthor of the PLAID for intermediate accounting, is also a coauthor of a leading text in intermediate accounting and has taught the subject matter for many years. Dr. Harrison is extensively engaged in teaching and research in financial accounting.

The user will find the coverage to be "student oriented" in that the essential subject matter is presented in a concise, uncomplicated, and effective manner.

Roger H. Hermanson
Coordinating Editor

PREFACE

This Programmed Learning Aid was written in response to a need by several groups for a concise and especially designed source of review materials covering the subject matter. The two volumes comprising the PLAID for intermediate accounting are not designed to be used as a textbook in the subject but rather as supplements to any standard work. They are especially appropriate for study and review purposes on a self-study basis where time constraints are critical; thus, they are recommended especially for the following groups: college students enrolled in an intermediate accounting course, students starting a master's degree program in business administration, participants in executive development programs, individuals in business, and any other individual wishing to review the subject matter of intermediate accounting.

The subject matter is organized in a sequence that follows logically and in the order that is generally followed in most of the well-known intermediate accounting texts. Although the material generally should be approached sequentially by the beginner, those who are actively enrolled in a related course or are reviewing will find that the chapters can be studied on a selective basis since each one represents a complete unit. Each chapter has been developed so as to focus on and explain concisely the *significant* concepts and procedures so that the reader is not immersed in a bulk of detail.

The special features of this PLAID have been designed in response to the stated objectives, that is, to provide a concise, organized, and effective plan of study and review of the subject matter for the reader. To this end the PLAID incorporates the following special features:

1. Concise and direct explanations in each chapter of the fundamental concepts and procedures.
2. Short and to-the-point illustrations that utilize simple figures to enhance the understanding of basic concepts and procedures.
3. Careful identification of subject matter with appropriate captions and sub-captions.
4. Short chapters that can be reviewed in 40 to 55 minutes.
5. Programming of questions and answers for review so that the reader can evaluate his progress in the subject matter while he is reading each chapter. Several sets of programmed questions and answers will be found in each chapter.
6. A total of six examinations in the two volumes designed specifically to duplicate the types of questions utilized in most intermediate accounting courses. These examinations are classified by subject matter (chapters); they are challenging and thought provoking. The answers are provided; therefore, this aspect of the PLAID should be especially attractive to those readers who use it concurrently with registration in intermediate accounting.

7. Underscoring or italicizing of important distinctions and key words (phrases) in order to direct attention to specific points that may be overlooked by the reader.

8. In each volume a complete table of contents and an index to facilitate the location of specific subjects included in the PLAID.

Experience has suggested that utilization of a well-designed learning aid as a supplement to a textbook tends to increase the student's demonstrated grasp of the subject matter with a minimum of additional effort. Also it is a handy reference for refreshing one's memory on a specific topic or group of topics.

The authors welcome suggestions and constructive comments in respect to the materials and presentations included in this PLAID.

GLENN A. WELSCH
WALTER T. HARRISON, JR.

CONTENTS

Volume 1

Volume 2

chapter 1

INTRODUCTION

Accounting can be defined as an information processing system that is designed to (1) *capture* and *measure* the economic essence of events affecting an entity and (2) report the economic effects of those events to decision-makers. This definition focuses on the *measurement* and *communication* aspects of accounting; for accounting, in large part, serves the measurement function of business. Accounting is often characterized as the measurement arm of economics. Furthermore, the accounting function of business communicates to decision-makers the results of the measurement process.

The decision-makers who use accounting reports are many and varied. Examples are managers, investors, and governments. These decision-makers frequently need specialized reports. Intermediate accounting is concerned with *general-purpose* financial reports rather than internal reports such as the daily cash report that a cash manager may need. Thus the focus of this book is directed toward the general-purpose financial statements (balance sheet, income statement, and statement of changes in financial position) that profit-oriented corporations periodically (usually annually) present to the public.

Delineation of the objectives of the general-purpose financial statements represents one of the most vexing problems facing the accounting profession. One view holds that a primary objective of financial statements is to report on managers' *stewardship* responsibility to shareholders (reporting on past performance). Another view is that financial statements should provide information that decision-makers can use to make *predictions* about future economic consequences accruing from the entity's activities. A different dimension is the widespread belief that financial statements should meet the information needs of *sophisticated* decision-makers such as pension fund managers and other institutional investors. Others believe that the primary purpose of financial statements should be to meet the less sophisticated information needs of *lay investors*. This issue will probably never be resolved; rather it illustrates the dynamic nature of the market for accounting information and presents a multifaceted challenge to aspiring young accountants to (1) identify relevant decision-makers, (2) identify their information needs, and (3) devise ways to meet those needs.

At the present time (spring 1977), the consensus appears to be that the objectives of financial statements are:

(1) To provide information useful for making economic decisions.
(2) To serve primarily those users who have limited authority, ability, or resources to obtain information and who rely on financial statements as their principal source of information about an enterprise's economic activities.
(3) To provide information useful to investors and creditors for predicting, comparing, and evaluating potential cash flows in terms of amount, timing, and related uncertainty.
(4) To provide users with information for predicting, comparing, and evaluating enterprise earning power.
(5) To supply information useful in judging management's ability to use enterprise resources effectively in achieving the primary enterprise goal.
(6) To provide factual and interpretative information about transactions and other events which is useful for predicting, comparing, and evaluating enterprise earning power. Basic underlying assumptions with respect to matters subject to interpretation, evaluation, prediction, or estimation should be disclosed.[1]

This quote makes it clear that the predictive objective of financial statements has been elevated to a reasonably high level of importance. The predictive objective is by its very nature future oriented. This is contrasted with the stewardship-reporting objective, which by nature is past oriented. These two temporal orientations (past and future) become operational in considerations as to whether the accounting system should measure resources in terms of *historical* costs (which are past oriented), *market values* (which are current and future oriented), or *replacement costs* (which also are current and future oriented).

Presently the generally accepted accounting model measures resources in terms of historical costs, although there are certain instances in which market values and replacement costs are deemed to be appropriate valuation bases. These exceptions to the historical-cost model are covered in this book. Also, Chapters 24 and 25 of Volume II of this series cover, in some detail, *alternative accounting models* that have been proposed as alternatives to the historical-cost model. In order to understand those models and more importantly to be able to function in the contemporary institutional environment, it is necessary to have a firm grasp of the accounting model currently in use. Therefore, this series is devoted substantially to coverage of the historical-cost model.

Generally Accepted Accounting Principles

The body of accounting knowledge which is germane to the contemporary accounting model is known as *generally accepted accounting principles (GAAP)*. GAAP are formulated by the Financial Accounting Standards Board, which has had this responsibility since 1973. During the period 1959–73, responsibility for establishing principles of accounting rested with the Accounting Principles Board of the American Institute of Certified Public Accountants (AICPA). Prior to that time, the Committee on Accounting Procedure of the AICPA established GAAP. It is worthy of note that the Accounting Principles Board and the Committee on Accounting Procedure were both elements of the AIPCA. By contrast, membership to the FASB is appointed by the trustees of an autonomous body, the Financial Accounting Foundation. Therefore, while the FASB is heavily influenced by the practicing accounting profession, it nevertheless is organizationally autonomous and has members who are investment bankers, academicians, and private accountants as well as practicing Certified Public Accountants (CPAs). GAAP are to be found in the following:

1. *Accounting Research Bulletins* (1–51) of the Committee on Accounting Procedure,
2. *Accounting Principles Board Opinions* (1–31) of the APB,
3. *Financial Accounting Statements* of the FASB. To date 16 statements have been issued by the FASB.
4. Certain other publications by the AICPA.

Prior to issuance of an FASB *Statement,* the FASB customarily engages in a substantial amount of research which is made available to interested parties in the form of a *Discussion Memorandum.* Then after a reasonable period of time and *if* the FASB deems it appropriate, they issue an *Exposure Draft* of the *proposed* statement. The purpose of both of these public disclosures is to elicit comments from interested parties. Finally, after an appropriate exposure period and *if* the members of the FASB have reached a consensus as to (1) the need for a new FASB *Statement* and (2) the content of the *Statement,* they issue the formal document, an FASB *Statement,* which serves as one of the financial accounting and reporting "rules" of the profession. These FASB *Statements* are issued from time to time as conditions change and new types of transactions evolve and therefore as needs arise.

It is very important for you to recognize that accounting is a behavioral science—with many of the same difficulties in modeling human behavior that beset other behavioral disciplines such as economics, psychology, and sociology. As a result, GAAP must be responsive to changes in business conditions and events that mirror the behavioral aspects of business.

---

[1] AICPA, *Objectives of Financial Statements, Report of the Study Group on the Objectives of Financial Statements* (New York, October 1973), pp. 61–66 (adapted).

Accounting Institutions

1. The *American Institute of Certified Public Accountants* (AICPA) is the professional organization of CPAs in the United States. The AICPA serves a number of vital functions:

a. Professional research and literature such as the *Journal of Accountancy,* the *Accountants Index, Accounting Trends and Techniques,* and *Accounting Research Studies.*

b. Rule making for professional (CPA) auditors through *Statements on Auditing Procedures,* which are to the auditing profession what FASB statements are to financial accounting.

Thus, the AICPA serves as *the* clearinghouse of information for the practicing CPAs in the United States. Its membership is restricted to Certified Public Accountants, but members are not required to be in the public practice of accounting. That is, *CPAs* who are accounting educators, in government service, or are employed by other types of organizations are eligible for membership.

2. *State Societies of CPAs* operate in the various states to grant and administer CPA certificates to qualifying individuals. In general, the state societies draw their authority from enabling state legislation and are modeled rather closely after the AICPA.

3. The *FASB* was mentioned above as the rule-making body in financial accounting. In general, this is the only function served by the FASB. The FASB derives this authority from the AICPA and the SEC, which explicitly recognize the FASB as the rule-making body for financial accounting. In turn, the *AICPA's authority* or *enforcement* of the FASB's pronouncements (rules) rests with its (the AICPA's) ability to grant or deny membership in the AICPA as well as to expel members. This expulsion does not cause the violating party to cease to be a CPA; only the state that granted the violating party's CPA certificate can revoke the certificate. The point of this brief discussion is that the FASB establishes accounting principles but has no enforcement function or authority. The AICPA, state societies of CPAs, and the Securities and Exchange Commission share the enforcement responsibility.

4. The *Securities and Exchange Commission* (*SEC*) of the Treasury Department of the United States government has a legislative mandate (Securities Act of 1933 and Securities Exchange Act of 1934) to protect the interests of investors in corporations that issue their stock to the public at large. Thus, the SEC is empowered to dictate accounting policy in the United States. To date the SEC has met its charge by working closely with the private sector (AICPA and FASB). The SEC has the responsibility for overseeing (1) the issuance of shares of stock to the public in interstate commerce and (2) the operations of the stock exchanges, as well as the over-the-counter market for stocks. In general, the SEC's function is served if it can insure an acceptable level of *disclosure* of financial information by registrant corporations. The SEC's formal documents, which specify its rules, are (*a*) *Regulation S-X,* entitled "The Form and Content of Financial Statements," and (*b*) *Accounting Series Releases* (*ASRs*) which operate as amendments to *Regulation S-X*. To date around 200 *ASRs* have been issued by the SEC.

It is important to note that the SEC's rules apply specifically to the information which corporations, whose stocks are issued interstate (as opposed to intrastate), are required to file with the SEC in order to (1) issue their stock to the public (this document is known as a *registration statement*) and (2) keep their registration statement in force (this amounts to the filing of periodic updates to the registration statement via a number of *forms,* one of which is Form 10-K, which is very similar to the financial statements that corporations present to the public).

5. The *American Accounting Association* (*AAA*) is an organization dominated by accounting educators; however, its membership is open to other accountants as well. Because of its academic orientation, the AAA's principal activities relate to accounting research. The AAA publishes *The Accounting Review,* which is devoted substantially to research articles in all areas of accounting (financial, managerial, taxation, auditing, etc.). The AAA operates through committees to shape the future of accounting thought. For example, a committee of the AAA issued in 1966 "A Statement of Basic Accounting Theory," and AAA committees and subcommittees respond regularly to FASB discussion memoranda and exposure drafts. Although the AAA has no rule-making function nor enforcement authority, it exerts significant influence through the research studies it sponsors, *The Accounting Review,* and other of its publications and activities.

chapter 2

THEORETICAL FOUNDATIONS OF FINANCIAL ACCOUNTING AND REPORTING

Frame 1[2]

Nature of Accounting Theory

Students who attempt to learn accounting by memorization of entries, computational approaches, and mechanics will experience difficulty. Alternatively, an understanding in depth of the *foundation of accounting theory* will place the student in a position to resolve new and complex situations (and problems) and to discuss points at issue effectively. You are urged to repeatedly return to this chapter to find the rationale for the discussions throughout this volume. The accounting profession—through such organizations as the American Institute of Certified Public Accountants, the American Accounting Association, the Financial Executives Institute (primarily accountants working for industry), and the National Association of Accountants (a varied membership)—is expending substantial amounts of money and effort in accounting research to (*a*) improve accounting theory and practice and (*b*) make information more useful to decision-makers.

In dealing with accounting theory one encounters a serious terminology problem; throughout accounting literature there are numerous references to accounting theory in the following terms: principles; concepts; conventions; doctrines; standards; rules; underlying assumptions; procedures; and postulates. Although each term is subject to precise definition, general usage has served to give them loose and overlapping meanings. In studying accounting at this level, it is imperative that some structure to accounting theory be provided. Accordingly, in order to establish a basis for organized study, the following frame of reference (structure) and terminology have been selected. As the student studies the various chapters, it may be observed that most of "accounting" can be explained in terms of this structure.

A Broad Structure of Financial Accounting and Reporting

1. Underlying environmental assumptions.
   a. The separate-entity assumption.
   b. The continuity assumption.
   c. The unit-of-measure assumption.
   d. The time-period assumption.
2. Basic accounting principles.
   a. The cost principle.

  b. The revenue principle.
  c. The matching principle.
  d. The objectivity principle.
  e. The consistency principle.
  f. The financial reporting principle.
  g. The exception principle:
    (1) Materiality.
    (2) Conservatism.
    (3) Industry peculiarities.
3. Implementing measurement principles.
  a. Selection of the objects, activities, and events to be measured.
  b. Identification and classification of the attributes of each object, activity, and event to be measured.
  c. Assignment of quantitative amounts to the attributes.
  d. Modifying measurement principle:
    (1) Uncertainty.
    (2) Objectivity.
    (3) Limitations of monetary unit.
    (4) Cost effectiveness.
4. Basic concepts of the accounting model.
  a. Assets = Liabilities + Owners' Equity.
  b. Net Income = Revenues − Expenses.
  c. Changes in Resources = Resource Inflows − Resource Outflows.
5. Implementing Accounting Principles and Procedures.
  a. Those related to determination of net income.
  b. Those related to measurement of assets and liabilities.
  c. Those related to recording transactions and other events.
  d. Those related to presentation of accounting information.

In the pages to follow, each of the above categories will be discussed.

Underlying Environmental Assumptions. The *four* underlying assumptions do not represent accounting; rather they are broad and relevant aspects of the *total environment* in which accounting necessarily operates, and they directly influence accounting theory and practice. The *separate-entity assumption* serves to define the boundaries of the individual economic unit (the business unit) for which accounting takes place; more directly, it identifies the individual business unit as separate and apart from the owners. Thus, the sole proprietorship, the partnership, and the corporation are each viewed as an accounting entity separate and apart from the specific owners thereof, despite the fact that this distinction may not be made by law. Personal transactions (as opposed to business transactions) do not enter into the accounting for the business unit.

The *continuity* assumption (frequently referred to as the going-concern concept) implies continuance of the business unit over a future period long enough to enable the entity to carry out contemplated activities; that is, the business is not expected to liquidate in the foreseeable future, and thus accounting is on a "nonliquidation" basis. This assumption underlies many of the cost valuations and other allocations common in accounting, such as depreciation.

The *unit-of-measure assumption* holds that the results of business transactions will be recorded and reported in the monetary unit of the nation. Of course, business executives impose this requirement and, as a consequence, the accounting profession must accept it. The monetary unit thus becomes the measurement device. Since the value of the monetary unit (dollar) changes (e.g., inflation involves a reduction in the value of the dollar; i.e., it will command less real goods), serious measurement problems arise. For example, a building purchased 20 years ago at a cost of $100,000 and depreciated to, say, $20,000 on the books may be worth $125,000 today simply due to inflationary effects. Nevertheless under the unit-of-measure assumption, changes in the value of the monetary unit (inflation and deflation) are disregarded; that is, the monetary unit is assumed to be *stable* in real value.

The *time-period assumption* recognizes that business executives (and all readers of financial statements) have a need for timely financial information. Although the results of operations of a business enterprise cannot be determined with precision until its final liquidation, interim (monthly, quarterly, and annual) financial statements are necessary. Again, accounting has no choice but to meet this vital need. The time-period assumption underlies the whole area of accounting accruals and deferrals which significantly affect the income statement, balance sheet, and statement of changes in financial position.

Basic Accounting Principles. These are the broad working rules of accounting action developed and accepted by the profession. These are the individual "generally accepted accounting principles" discussed in Chapter 1. They are developed (and revised) in response to the business environment and the specific needs of the users of accounting information. To be "generally accepted" the concept must have the substantial authoritative support of the accounting profession. The *seven* generally accepted accounting principles listed on pages 4 and 5 are discussed below.

The Cost Principle. The cost principle holds that *cost* is the appropriate basis for initial accounting recognition (recording at date of acquisition) of all asset acquisitions, service acquisitions, expenses, costs, creditor equities, and owner equities. The principle recognizes completed business transactions as the basic unit of analysis of accounting; the transactions are analyzed and recorded in terms of their economic effect (in dollars) on the business unit. In applying the cost principle, frequently there is a serious problem of *determining* cost when noncash considerations are involved. In such cases, the cost measure (assuming an arm's-length transaction) is the cash equivalent (fair market value) of the consideration given up or the cash equivalent of the economic item acquired, whichever is the more clearly evident.

The Revenue Principle. The revenue principle defines revenue and specifies the point in time that revenue should be recognized in the accounting records. Revenue is broadly defined as the creation of goods or services by an enterprise for a specific interval of time. As such, revenue is also properly viewed as the net asset increase from (*a*) the sales of goods and services; (*b*) interest, rent, royalties, and so forth, received; (*c*) net gain on the sale of assets other than stock in trade; and (*d*) gain from the advantageous settlement of liabilities. As to timing, the principle generally holds that revenue should be recognized in the accounts when it is *realized*. Realization of sales revenue is considered to occur when title to the goods passes; realization of service revenue occurs when the service is rendered. In recent years the revenue principle has been modified to include *unrealized* net asset increases and decreases in a limited number of instances.

The Matching Principle. This principle holds that for any period for which net income is to be determined and reported, the revenues and all of the expired costs that generated that revenue must be matched and reported for that period. If revenue is carried over from a prior period or deferred to a future period in accordance with the revenue principle, all elements of cost that are related to that revenue likewise must be carried over, that is, accrued or deferred, as the case may be. The matching principle often requires that the accountant deal with estimates (such as the estimated cost of warranties on goods sold).

The Objectivity Principle. This principle holds that to the fullest extent possible accounting should be based on objective data. In recording and reporting the results of transactions, accounting should look to completed transactions resulting from bargaining between parties having adverse interests (arm's-length transactions). To the fullest extent possible, accounting data must be supported by formal and verifiable business documents originating outside the entity. Under this principle, opinions, estimates, and judgmental decisions are used only when more objective data are not available.

The Consistency Principle. This principle holds that for each company there must be a consistent application of accounting principles from one period to the next. Consistent accounting for the entity should be followed so that the resulting financial data are comparable from period to period. The consistency principle does not preclude changes in accounting to improve the measurement and reporting. When changes in accounting are desirable for sound reasons, a description of the change and the dollar effect should be disclosed on the financial statements in order to facilitate interperiod comparisons.

The Financial Reporting Principle. This principle holds that there must be complete and understandable reporting on the financial statements of all significant information relating to the economic activities of the entity. The degree of disclosure must be such that the financial statements will not be misleading. The principle is especially applicable to unusual events and major changes. It may involve additional information in the body of the statement or by extended explanations in footnotes to the statements.

The Exception Principle. Accounting principles must be pragmatic in order to apply to diverse situations. The exception principle recognizes this fact and provides for the needed flexibility. The exception principle states that there are situations where specific exceptions to the other accounting principles may be permitted. It includes three fairly specific concepts that have been widely recognized and accepted in accounting practice, viz:

1. *Materiality.* This concept holds that items of small significance as to amount need not be accorded strict theoretical treatment. An item is considered not material if knowledge of it would not alter the decision of a prudent decision-maker.
2. *Conservatism.* This concept, as applied in accounting, holds that where alternatives for an accounting determination are possible, each having some reasonable support, that alternative having the *least favorable immediate impact* on the owners' equity should be selected. Thus, where there is a choice to be made, the concept would favor understating assets and income as opposed to overstating them.
3. *Industry Peculiarities.* In view of the concern of accounting for usefulness, feasibility, and appropriateness, the peculiarities of an industry (not an individual company) may justify certain exceptions to accounting principles and practices. The exception principle provides for a special accounting for specific items where there is a clear precedent in the industry, based on objective need, rationale, and feasibility. It is appropriate also to note that some aspects of accounting are in response to legal requirements; this is especially true with respect to certain state laws relating to corporate capital.

Check your progress by marking each of the following questions as T or F. It may be necessary to refer back to Chapter 1.

——— 1. Accounting is much like the natural sciences in that it is governed by natural universal laws similar to gravity and the speed of sound, which are invariant across entities and time.

——— 2. The underlying environmental assumptions are not only a part of the accounting environment but also are expressions of assumptions made about broad economic phenomena.

——— 3. The unit-of-measure assumption effectively ignores price inflation and deflation.

——— 4. The basic accounting principles constitute what is generally accepted for current practice.

——— 5. The matching principle can be construed to embody both the revenue and the cost principles.

——— 6. The consistency principle dictates that firms should not make changes in their accounting methods.

Now check your responses by referring to Answer Frame 1², page 8.

Frame 2²

Implementing Measurement Principles. In Chapter 1 it was pointed out that accounting is concerned with measurement of business activities. Thus, there are a number of *implementing* measurement principles with which the accountant must deal at a theoretical level.

Answer frame 1²

1. False. Accounting is more like a behavioral science inasmuch as it attempts to model business *behavior*.
2. True. It is necessary to deal with the economic environment, and making certain assumptions facilitates this task.
3. True. Many view this as the primary weakness in the contemporary accounting model.
4. True. Virtually all rules of conduct in a free society derive their authority from the general acceptance of those who are affected by the rules. The same is true of the basic accounting principles.
5. True. Matching refers to the matching of costs against the related revenues. The revenue principle defines revenue, and the cost principle defines the relevant costs. Therefore, the matching principle embodies both the revenue and the cost principles.
6. False. For cases in which a change is needed to more realistically portray economic reality, an accounting change should be made. However, this provision should not be abused. Rather, every effort should be made to enable decision-makers to make interperiod comparisons.

If you missed any of the above, reread Frame 1² before beginning Frame 2², page 7.

Frame 2² continued

First, the accountant must determine which *objects, activities, and events* are to be measured. This determination is more fundamental than perhaps any other theoretical consideration, except for the identification of the hypothetical decision-maker whose information needs the accounting system is designed to meet. Examples of *objects* are assets and liabilities; examples of *activities* are sales of inventory and payments of dividends; examples of *events* are casualty losses, price-level changes, and wear and tear on machinery.

Second, the accountant must identify the salient *attributes* of the objects, activities, and events. An example of this identification process can be seen in the decision of which aspect of an advertising outlay to report. Possibilities are any one or a combination of (*a*) cash outlay, (*b*) advertising medium employed, (*c*) number of new customers expected as a result of the advertisement, (*d*) additional sales revenue expected to be generated from the outlay, and so forth. The accounting profession is vitally interested in new and feasible approaches to measuring and effectively reporting data such as these.

Third, the accountant generally deals with *quantitative amounts*. These may be stated in monetary or nonmonetary terms. For example, in the preceding paragraph, items (*a*), (*c*), and (*d*) are quantitative, while (*b*) is nonquantitative. Of the quantitative measures, (*a*) and (*d*) are monetary and (*c*) is nonmonetary. For most business applications, comparisons are essential to the evaluation process, so at least ordinal data (such as first, second, . . . , last) are needed. Moreover, cardinal data (such as 6.9, 125, etc.) make possible still finer comparisons. Finally, by stating most cardinal measures in dollar terms (a common denominator), ratios can be formed to permit even finer distinctions. For reasons such as these, much of the data with which accounting is concerned is stated in monetary terms.

Fourth, the accountant frequently must *constrain* the measurement process because it is necessary to assign measurements in an environment characterized by *uncertainty*. This uncertainty necessarily forces allocations of items like fixed asset costs (i.e., depreciation) to an estimated number of future periods over which the asset is expected to remain in service. Depreciation illustrates that there is considerable subjectivity in such allocations. In order to induce more *objectivity* into the accounting process, conventions are often adopted. Examples are the various systematic depreciation methods; they deal with an uncertain future and the consequent subjectivity by forcing objectivity into the measurement of periodic depreciation. In some cases, the need for objectivity impedes the accounting process.

Additional constraints on an optimal measurement process are caused by the fact that, contrary to the *unit-of-measure assumption,* the dollar does not have a constant purchasing power over time. Another constraint is due to the economic necessity that measurements be *cost efficient*. That is, some measurements may be "better" than others, but the marginal cost of obtaining the better measure may be greater than the marginal benefit. Thus, it is not cost efficient.

Basic Concepts of the Accounting Model. Three basic concepts are covered here, and each concept relates to one of the three primary financial statements.

The *financial position model* states that:

$$\text{Assets} = \text{Equities} \tag{1}$$

or

$$\text{Assets} = \text{Liabilities} + \text{Owners' Equity} \tag{2}$$

In simple terms the model (Equation 1) states that *all* the assets of an entity are owned by someone. That is, for every asset there are one or more equities (ownership rights). More specifically the model (Equation 2) states that the sum of the assets of an entity are owned by the creditors (to whom the liabilities are owed) and the owners of the entity (in the case of a corporation, evidenced by shares of stock). The financial position model is frequently referred to as the equation of the entity's statement of financial position, or *balance sheet*.

The *results of operations model* states that:

$$\text{Net Income for the Period} = \text{Revenues for the Period} - \text{Expenses for the Period} \tag{3}$$

This model is the equation of the *income statement*. It is less fundamental than the financial position model because all the elements of Equation 3 (revenues and expenses) are elements of *owners' equity* in Equation 2. That is, revenues are positive elements of owners' equity and expenses are negative elements of owners' equity. Therefore, we may combine Equations 2 and 3 as follows:

$$\text{Assets} = \text{Liabilities} + (\text{Owners' Equity} + \text{Revenues} - \text{Expenses}) \tag{4}$$

The *changes in financial position model* states that:

$$\text{Change in Resources} = \text{Resource Inflows} - \text{Resource Outflows} \tag{5}$$

Resources referred to in Equation 5 are construed very liberally to include all assets, liabilities, and elements of owners' equity. The vagueness of the term "resources" in this context should not be bothersome. Suffice it to say that the changes in financial position model is the equation of the third primary financial statement, the *statement of changes in financial position*. Furthermore, this model draws in large part from a number of conventions that will be explained more fully in Volume 2, Chapter 21, which is devoted to the statement of changes in financial position. Finally, it should not surprise the reader that the models of Equations 4 and 5 are interdependent; however, it is not expedient at this point to expound on the interrelationship.

Implementing Accounting Principles and Procedures. This section refers to the detailed implementation of principles and procedures to accounting for specific items such as receivables and rent expense. For any one item, the implementation process will likely encompass *income determination, measurement of assets or liabilities, the recording of transactions and events,* and *the presentation of accounting information.* These details of implementation comprise most of the remainder of this two-volume series.

In conclusion, the reader should retrace the path through this chapter from (1) underlying assumptions to (2) basic accounting principles to (3) implementing measurement principles to (4) basic concepts of the accounting model to (5) the notion of implementing the detailed principles and procedures. You will note that there is a natural progression from the abstract to the concrete, from the highly theoretical to the practical implementation of the concepts.

True or false?

_____ 1.   From the text discussion it appears that there is an adversary relationship between *uncertainty* in the accounting environment and the desire to present *objective* information.

_____ 2.   Quantitative information is always more useful than nonquantitative information.

_____ 3.   The statement that "Revenues exceed expenses for the period" implies an increase in net assets (assets less liabilities) for the period.

_____ 4.   The objects, activities, and events to be measured by an accounting system are established by precedent, which is not modified over time.

Now compare your responses with those given in Answer Frame 2², page 12.

chapter 3

REVIEW—THE ACCOUNTING MODEL AND INFORMATION PROCESSING

Frame 1³

The Accounting Model

First, recall that the accounting model (of Equation 4 from Chapter 2) may be written as:

$$\text{Assets} = \text{Liabilities} + \text{Owners' Equity} + \text{Revenues} - \text{Expenses}$$

This model reports financial position at a specific date; it does not report the *causes* of the *changes* in financial position that occurred *during the period*. The changes are recorded in terms of *assets, liabilities, owners' equity, revenues,* and *expenses*. This illustrates a fundamental fact of the general accounting model: there are only five types of accounts:

1.   Asset accounts.
2.   Liability accounts.
3.   Owners' equity (frequently referred to as *capital*) accounts.
4.   Revenue accounts.
5.   Expense accounts.

Therefore, the causes underlying the changes in financial position may be ascertained by analyzing the various accounts.

Each of the five categories of accounts has some unique characteristics that are common to all the individual accounts in that category. This commonality applies most directly to the manner of recording *increases* and *decreases* in all the accounts that represent the items within a category.

The manner of recording increases and decreases in accounts is known as the "rules of debit and credit," which literally means "left" and "right," respectively. Simply stated, the rules are that:

1. *Increases* in *assets* and *expenses* are recorded with debits; *decreases* are recorded with *credits*.
2. *Increases* in *liabilities,* items of *owners' equity,* and *revenues* are recorded with *credits; decreases* are recorded with *debits*.

Nature of the Accounting Process

The accounting process involves the following steps:

Step 1. Collection and Analysis of Raw Economic Data. First, of course, the data must be collected. This will often involve collection of business documents such as invoices, bank statements, and contracts. Second, the data must be analyzed pursuant to determining how it is to be recorded. Generally speaking, there are two types of events that must be recorded: (1) external transactions executed with outsiders— for example, sales, purchases, payments and receipts of cash—usually supported by formal documents such as an invoice and (2) other events which are *not* transactions but which exert an economic impact on the business, such as depreciation of fixed assets and the accrual of unpaid wage expense. This analysis is the most intellectually stimulating and the most critical of the accounting process, for it determines how an event is to be recorded.

Step 2. Recording (Journalizing) the Economic Data. Both types of events referred to above are recorded in the journal (book of *original* entry) in chronological order so as to reflect a "running record" of the effects of the events on the company's financial position, results of operations, and the changes in its financial position. Customarily there is one *general journal* and also a series of *special journals,* such as the sales, purchases, cash receipts, and cash disbursements journals. Special journals save time because they facilitate the handling of a larger number of identical transactions.

Step 3. Transferring Amounts from the Journals to the Ledger (Posting). The ledger essentially contains a separate account for each item of revenue and expense, and for each asset, liability, and owners' equity component. The amounts are posted from the journal to the ledger (book of *final* entry) where the data are collected by account. The ledger may contain some *control accounts* each of which is supported by a detailed *subsidiary ledger,* such as the accounts receivable control account that is supported by the accounts receivable subsidiary ledger.

Step 4. Preparation of an Unadjusted Trial Balance. At the end of the accounting period (or when financial statements are desired), a trial balance is prepared to prove the *mechanical* accuracy of the ledger and to provide data for the subsequent steps. The subsidiary ledgers are also verified for agreement with their respective control accounts.

Step 5. Preparation of a Worksheet. The accountant's worksheet starts with the unadjusted trial balance (step 4) and incorporates *adjusting entries* to reflect changes in expense, revenue, asset, and liability accounts that result from events other than external transactions. Examples are salaries owed, depreciation, and interest earned but not received. The worksheet generally reflects a debit and a credit column for each of the following: trial balance, adjustments, adjusted trial balance, income statement, and balance sheet. When completed, the worksheet provides data for the (*a*) income statement, (*b*) balance sheet, (*c*) adjusting journal entries, and (*d*) the closing entries.

Step 6. Preparation of Financial Statements. These are based on data provided by the worksheet.

Step 7. Preparation of Adjusting Entries and Closing Entries. Adjusting and closing entries are journalized from the worksheet and posted.

Answer frame 2²

1. True. This adversary relationship is clearly seen in the terms "uncertainty" and "objective." Uncertainty is inherent with respect to future events. Measurement of future events is inherently subjective. The past is known with certainty, and hence measurements of the past are objective. The application to accounting has to do with decision-makers' overall need for objective information about an uncertain future. This overall need is impossible to fill. Therefore, a second-best solution must be found: either subjective information about the future or objective information about the past. Heretofore, the latter solution has been offered by the accounting profession.

2. False. The statement as written ignores *relevance* as a criterion. For example, it may be more useful for purposes of predicting future success to know that Company X has employed a distinguished individual as its president than to know the company's net income for the past year. In general, however, quantitative information is more useful because of the ease it affords for making comparisons.

3. True. "Net assets" is another name for owners' equity. Because revenues are positive elements of owners' equity and expenses are negative elements of owners' equity, an excess of revenues over expenses implies an increase in owners' equity, which is equivalent to an increase in net assets.

4. False. The objects, activities, and events are established essentially by precedent, but they must be modified over time to reflect current economic reality. In this respect accounting is very much like the other professions. Examples of *changing activities* were a number of new methods during the 1960s of combining corporations.

If you missed any of the above, reread Frame 2² before beginning Chapter 3.

Frame 1³ continued

Step 8. Preparation of a Postclosing Trial Balance. This step is taken as proof of the mechanical accuracy of steps 5–7.

Step 9. Reversing Entries. Reversing entries are made, *if desirable,* as of the first day of the next period.

Indicate whether each of the following statements is true or false by writing *T* or *F* in the space provided.

_____ 1. The main function of the rules of debit and credit is to identify the various economic effects caused by each transaction.

_____ 2. The general and special journals serve as the chronological record of an entity's transactions.

_____ 3. The general ledger contains all the asset, liability, owners' equity, revenue, and expense accounts, as well as the monetary balance in each individual account.

_____ 4. Adjusting entries should be made on the worksheet prior to preparation of the financial statements.

Answers are given in Answer Frame 1³, page 14.

Frame 2[3]

Adjusting Entries

At the end of the accounting period some of the balances in the ledger (as shown in the trial balance) may not reflect the correct amount (on an accrual basis) of revenue, expense, assets, or liabilities as the case may be. Thus, certain internal events must be given recognition through *adjusting entries* so that the financial statements will reflect correct amounts. Data for adjusting entries usually must be generated internally; data may be needed for the following kinds of adjustments:

a. Merchandise inventory.
b. Prepaid expenses.
c. Accrued expenses.
d. Unearned (prepaid) revenues.
e. Accrued revenues.
f. Estimated items.

Each of these types of adjustments will be reviewed and illustrated.

Merchandise Inventory.   Assuming periodic inventory procedures, the valuation of the ending inventory must be determined; then an adjusting entry must be made for both the beginning and ending inventory values. To illustrate, the adjusting entries for a trading company would be:

1. To transfer the valuation of the *beginning* inventory to the Income Summary (or alternatively to the Cost of Goods Sold) account:

Income summary (or cost of goods sold)	5,000	
Merchandise inventory		5,000

2. To record the valuation of the *ending* inventory:

Merchandise inventory	7,000	
Income summary (or cost of goods sold)		7,000

Alternatively, the two entries above could be combined into only one entry with the same effect because the Merchandise Inventory account in both entries is the same account. The combined entry would be:

Merchandise inventory	2,000	
Income summary (or cost of goods sold)		2,000

Prepaid Expenses.   These entries recognize the effect of expenses (goods or services) paid in advance of their consumption (utilization) through operations. To illustrate, assume a three-year insurance premium (on property) of $600 was paid on January 1, 19A; the adjusting entry on December 31, 19A, would be:

a. Assuming the original entry debited Insurance Expense for $600:

Prepaid insurance (⅔ × $600)	400	
Insurance expense		400

b. Alternatively, had the original debit of $600 been to Prepaid Insurance, the adjusting entry would have been:

Insurance expense (⅓ × $600)	200	
Prepaid insurance		200

Accrued Expenses.   These are expenses incurred but not paid and not yet recorded at the end of the accounting period. To illustrate, assuming wages amounting to $4,500 for the last three days of December 19A were not paid (nor yet recorded) on December 31, 19A, the adjusting entry would be:

Wage expense	4,500	
Wages payable		4,500

Answer frame 1³

1. False. The rules of debit and credit serve as a measure of recording increases and decreases in the various types of accounts.
2. True. All transactions are recorded in the general journal as well as in the special journals, in order of date.
3. True. All of the individual accounts are included in the general ledger, and the economic effects of all transactions and other recordable events are transferred to it.
4. True. Adjusting entries should be made on the worksheet which is completed *prior* to the preparation of the financial statements because the effects of adjusting entries must be reflected in the account balances that are reported in the financial statements.

If you missed any of the above, reread Frame 1³ before beginning Frame 2³, page 13.

Frame 2³ continued

Unearned (Prepaid) Revenues. This is revenue collected in advance of being earned; consequently, unearned revenues are liabilities. To illustrate, assume rent of $2,400 was collected on November 1, 19A, for the following 12 months; the adjusting entry at December 31, 19A, would be:

a. Assuming the original entry credited the $2,400 to Unearned Rent Revenue:

Unearned rent revenue ($2,400 × $\frac{2}{12}$)	400	
Rent revenue ($2,400 × $\frac{10}{12}$)		400

b. Assuming the original entry credited the $2,400 to Rent Revenue:

Rent revenue ($2,400 × $\frac{10}{12}$)	2,000	
Unearned rent revenue		2,000

Accrued Revenues. This is revenue earned by the end of the accounting period but not yet collected (nor yet recorded) at the end of the period. To illustrate, assuming interest revenue for four months on a $1,000, 6% note receivable had not been collected (nor recorded) on December 31, 19A, the adjusting entry at that date would be:

Interest receivable	20	
Interest revenue ($1,000 × 6% × $\frac{4}{12}$)		20

Estimated Items. It is common for companies to have to estimate certain items of expense. Such estimates are based on historical experience and related future expectations. Examples are depreciation expense and bad debt expense. To illustrate depreciation, assume that a machine cost $10,000 on January 1, 19A, and was expected to remain in service for five years, at which time it could be sold as scrap for $1,000. The depreciation adjusting entry for each year (19A–19E) would be:

Depreciation expense [($10,000 − $1,000) ÷ 5]	1,800	
Accumulated depreciation—machinery		1,800

To illustrate bad debt expense, assume a company's credit sales for a period were $20,000 and that the expected loss rate is 2% of credit sales. Under these conditions, the adjusting entry to record Bad Debt Expense for the year would be:

Bad debt expense ($20,000 × .02)	400	
Allowance for doubtful accounts		400

Closing Entries

After the ledger accounts have been adjusted (i.e., adjusting journal entries have been posted), and the financial statements prepared, the *nominal accounts* (income statement accounts) must be closed. This is necesasry because the income statement accounts (revenues and expenses) relate *only* to a specific interval of time. Therefore, it is necessary at the end of each period to "close" the balances in these accounts to make them zero. The interrelationship of the income statement and balance sheet is manifested by the fact that the net effect of all revenues and expenses (net income) for a period is closed to the Retained Earnings account, which is an element of Owners' Equity, which in turn is a *real* account (balance sheet account).The closing medium is known as "closing entries"; they are entered in the general journal and then posted to the ledger. Typical closing entries at the end of the accounting period for a trading company would be:

a. To close the revenue accounts:

Sales revenue	100,000	
Interest revenue	20	
Gain on sale of fixed assets	100	
Income summary		100,120

b. To close the expense accounts:

Income summary	89,400	
Cost of goods sold		56,400
Administrative expenses		8,100
Selling (distribution) expenses		15,100
Interest expense		200
Income tax expense		9,600

c. To close the Income Summary account to Retained Earnings:

Income summary ($100,120 − $89,400)	10,720	
Retained earnings		10,720

Reversing Entries

This procedure, frequently referred to as readjusting the ledger, is strictly an optional step; the accountant can choose to "reverse" certain entries or not as preferred. Reversing entries are made to accomplish only one purpose, that is, to *facilitate subsequent entries* to the account(s) involved. To illustrate, assume the adjusting entry (given above) for accrued wages was made on December 31, 19A. To repeat it, for convenience the adjusting entry was:

Wage expense (unpaid wages for the last three days of December 19A)	4,500	
Wages payable		4,500

a. Now assume the above adjusting entry is *not reversed;* when wages are paid on January 15, 19B, the following entry must be made (wages for the last three days of 19A must be separately identified):

Wages payable	4,500	
Wage expense (19B)	19,500	
Cash		24,000

b. Alternatively, now assume the above adjusting entry *was reversed* by means of the following reversing entry dated January 1, 19B:

Wages payable	4,500	
Wage expense		4,500

Then, it follows that the entry on January 15, 19B, for payment of wages would be as follows (note that wages for the last three days of 19A need not be separately identified):

Wage expense	24,000	
Cash		24,000

Note that the Wage Expense account in both instances will have a balance of $19,500 for 19B after the payment of $24,000 on January 15, 19B. Also note that in both instances, $4,500 of the total expense is properly allocated to 19A.

This review summarizes the entire accounting process from collection of the raw data through preparation of the financial statements to adjusting, closing, and reversing entries (steps 1–9). However, it only considers in any detail the adjusting, closing, and reversing entries. This is because such steps as posting and the worksheet are covered in most elementary accounting texts, and preparation and content of the financial statements are covered in Chapters 4, 5, and 21.

True or false?

_____ 1. In general, the purpose of making adjusting entries is to allocate to accounting periods the correct amount of revenue and expense.

_____ 2. The purpose of making closing entries is very similar to the purpose of making adjusting entries.

_____ 3. Closing entries are optional, whereas adjusting entries and reversing entries are essential.

_____ 4. The following entry is an example of an adjusting entry:

```
Sales revenue  . . . . . . . . . . . . . . . .    500
     Income summary  . . . . . . . . . . . . .          500
```

_____ 5. If $1,000 were paid for supplies and immediately debited to the asset account, Supplies, then the year-end adjusting entry

```
Supplies expense  . . . . . . . . . . . . . .    400
     Supplies  . . . . . . . . . . . . . . . .          400
```

implies that $600 of the supplies is on hand at year-end.

Now check your responses by comparing them to Answer Frame 2³, page 18.

chapter 4

REVIEW—THE INCOME STATEMENT AND RETAINED EARNINGS

Frame 1[4]

In Chapters 1–3, considerable attention was focused on the *financial statements*. This chapter reviews one of the three primary financial statements, the *income statement,* as well as retained earnings. The income statement and retained earnings are closely related because the net income from the income statement of each accounting period is "closed" into the Retained Earnings account of the balance sheet. Chapter 5 will review the other two primary financial statements, the balance sheet and the statement of changes in financial position (SCFP).

The diagram below shows the relationship among the three primary financial statements—for one accounting period. (The statement of retained earnings is viewed by many as supplementary.)

Beginning Balance Sheet +	Income Statement for the Period +	Statement of Retained Earnings[1] + for the Period	Statement of Changes in Financial Position for the Period	Ending = Balance Sheet

Note in particular that the beginning and ending balance sheets are snapshot pictures of the assets and the equities of the entity at *two points in time*. The income statement, the retained earnings statement, and the SCFP all cover a *period of time;* thus, they present *reasons* for the changes in the entity's ending assets and equities vis-à-vis the beginning assets and equities. The changes in assets and equities that arise from *revenues* and *expenses* (that appear on the period's income statement) are the subject of this chapter.

Basic Definitions

Before we launch into a discussion of the income statement, we need to define the elements of the income statement. These definitions are mere skeletons of the complete definitions, but they capture the essence of each key term.

1. Revenue—increase in resources resulting from the major activities of the enterprise; a few examples are sales revenue, rent revenue, interest revenue, and laundry service revenue.

---

[1] Many companies present a statement of owners' equity, which includes Retained Earnings and the other owners' equity accounts such as Common Stock, Preferred Stock, and Other Contributed Capital.

Answer frame 2³

1. True. The purpose of adjusting entries is to reflect economic *changes* in certain revenue and expense accounts that have not yet been specifically recorded.
2. False. The purpose of making *closing* entries is to zero out the balances in the *income statement* accounts pursuant to beginning the accounting process for the next period.
3. False. Reversing entries are optional. Adjusting and closing entries are deemed to be essential.
4. False. The entry given is an example of a *closing* entry—made to close (or zero out) a *credit* balance of $500 in the Sales Revenue account.
5. True. Note that the acquisition, debited to the *Supplies* account for $1,000, created a $1,000 debit balance in the account. Then the $400 adjusting entry given in the question *credited* the Supplies account for $400, leaving a $600 debit balance in the account (assuming there was no beginning balance in the supplies account).

If you missed any of the above questions, you should reread Frame 2³ before proceeding. Then continue reading with Chapter 4.

Frame 1⁴ continued

2. Income (or earnings)—a difference, that is, revenue minus expense; examples are *income* before income tax and *net income.*
3. Expense—*expired* assets (or expired costs); that is, assets used up in the earning process; examples are the cost of goods sold, salary expense, depreciation expense, and insurance expense.
4. Cost—the measure of resources given up to acquire other resources. Costs may be *expired* or *unexpired. Unexpired* costs apply to *assets* (which are purchased) such as merchandise inventory, supplies, and buildings. *Expired* costs apply to *expenses;* examples are given above.
5. Gains and losses—net revenues and net expenses, respectively, resulting from dispositions of assets or settlements of debts, such items being only indirectly related to the enterprise's major activities; examples are a gain on sale of building and a loss on retirement of bonds payable.

Concepts of Income

Economists define *income* as the maximum amount that an owner of a business can remove from the business during a period of time and leave the business exactly as well off as it was at the beginning of the period. Or, it is the *increase* in the present value[2] of the owners' equity of the business, adjusted for withdrawals and additional contributions of capital made by owners of the business. This theoretical definition is the *ideal.* Unfortunately, it cannot be measured with a high degree of precision because present value computations require specification of (1) future cash flows, which are uncertain, and (2) a discount rate of earnings, which is also subject to change and other elements of uncertainty.

Accountants have developed *accounting income* as a surrogate for economic income. Accounting income is the excess of realized revenues over actual expenses for a period of time. The revenue and cost principles are employed to measure revenues and expenses, and the matching principle is the basis for matching expenses against revenues to arrive at net income of the period. This process represents an attempt to match resources consumed (expenses) against resources created (revenues) and hence measure the increase in owners' equity for the period. Notice the past tense of the verbs "consumed" and "created" in the preceding sentence. This indicates that accounting income is, in general, past oriented, whereas economic income is current and future oriented. The reason for this dichotomy is that financial statement users have heretofore required a high level of precision with respect to the information presented therein.

[2] Present (and future) value concepts are covered in Chapter 6.

This precision can only be achieved by basing the accounting model on past-oriented values (i.e., historical costs).

The demand for precision in financial reporting has diminished considerably within the last few years due in large part to persistently high rates of inflation, which have reduced the usefulness of historical-cost financial statements. As a result, the accounting profession is giving much attention to alternative models of accounting as possible alternatives or outright replacements for the model in use today. And the Securities and Exchange Commission began in 1976 to require very large companies to disclose in their filings with the Commission, the *current replacement costs* of key assets and expenses as supplements to the historical-cost financial statements. Thus, it appears that the gap between economic income and accounting income may be narrowing. The most frequently mentioned alternative accounting models are covered in Chapters 24 and 25 of Volume 2 of this series.

Importance of the Income Statement

The income statement is generally regarded as the most important of the three primary financial statements because it presents the entity's net income for the period. Net income derives its importance from the fact that most of the theoretical models used (in finance) to predict the market value of a company's stock rely on net income or some derivative thereof (such as dividends) as the most important variable in the prediction. This is not surprising since net income synthesizes the results of all the enterprise's operations for the period. As such, it embodies *all* the revenues and *all* the expenses of the entity for the period. Therefore, it is crucially important that net income be measured as accurately as possible. Equally important is the need to disclose enough additional information to enable financial statement users to intelligently *interpret* net income.

The need for this interpretative information is evident from the recent increase in the amount and the sophistication of footnote disclosures in the financial statements. For example, an investor who is comparing two companies of roughly equal size and in the same industry may find that both companies have equal amounts of long-term debt. But a closer examination of the footnotes may reveal that Company A has a substantially larger interest burden (higher interest rates) than Company B. Furthermore, the "Lease Agreement" footnote may uncover that Company A has a number of long-term noncancelable lease liabilities that do not appear in the columnar list of balance sheet liabilities. The analyst may decide on this basis to make some "adjustments" to the *reported net income* of these two companies to place them on a comparable footing prior to making predictions of the companies' stock values.

Many other examples could be used to illustrate the importance of the income statement in financial analysis. These same examples would underscore the complexities which are inherent in measuring periodic income.

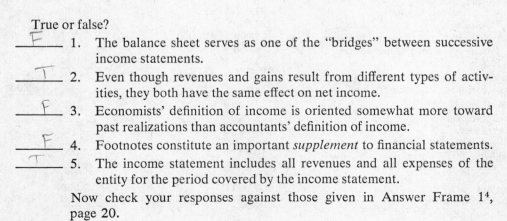

True or false?

_____ F _____ 1.   The balance sheet serves as one of the "bridges" between successive income statements.

_____ T _____ 2.   Even though revenues and gains result from different types of activities, they both have the same effect on net income.

_____ F _____ 3.   Economists' definition of income is oriented somewhat more toward past realizations than accountants' definition of income.

_____ F _____ 4.   Footnotes constitute an important *supplement* to financial statements.

_____ T _____ 5.   The income statement includes all revenues and all expenses of the entity for the period covered by the income statement.

Now check your responses against those given in Answer Frame 1⁴, page 20.

Answer frame 1⁴

1. False. The income statement serves as one of the "bridges" between successive balance sheets. The other "bridges" are the SCFP and the statement of retained earnings.
2. True. Both represent operating *increments* to net assets; hence they both increase net income.
3. False. The opposite is true. Economic income is more *future oriented* than accounting income.
4. False. Footnotes are a part of (not "supplement to") financial statements.
5. True. This is the nature and purpose of the income statement.

If you missed any of the above, reread Frame 1⁴ before beginning Frame 2⁴, below.

Frame 2⁴

The discussion of Frame 1⁴ was largely conceptual. In this frame we turn our attention exclusively to the income statement (and the statement of retained earnings) of the historical-cost accounting model. Thus, we are dealing with statements that reflect realized revenues and expired (historical) costs. Illustration 4–1 below is an example of an income statement and a retained earnings statement. The illustration will be used throughout this frame to highlight certain key points pertaining to these financial statements.

Illustration 4–1

SAMPLE COMPANY, INCORPORATED
Income Statements for the Years Ended December 31, 19B and 19C

	19B			19C		
Revenues:						
Gross sales		$382,000			$403,000	
Less: Sales returns and allowances	$ 7,000			$ 7,500		
Sales discounts	4,000	11,000		4,500	12,000	
Net Sales			$371,000			$391,000
Costs and expenses:						
Cost of goods sold:						
Merchandise inventory, beginning	83,000			90,000		
Add: Purchases	228,000			235,000		
Freight-in	8,000	319,000		8,500	333,500	
Less: Purchase returns and allowances . . .	4,000			4,500		
Purchase discounts	3,000	7,000		4,000	8,500	
Total goods available for sale		312,000			325,000	
Deduct: Merchandise inventory, ending . . .		90,000			95,000	
Cost of goods sold			222,000			230,000
Gross margin on sales			149,000			161,000
Operating expenses:						
Distribution expenses:						
Advertising	10,000			12,000		
Sales	64,000			66,000		
Commissions	4,000			4,500		
Freight-out	7,000			7,000		
Other distribution expenses	6,000	91,000		7,000	96,500	

Illustration 4–1 (*continued*)

	19B			19C		
General and administrative expenses:						
Office expenses	8,000			7,500		
Office payroll	23,200			23,500		
Amortization of patent	800			1,000		
Depreciation on store equipment	2,000			2,000		
Bad debt expense	3,000			2,500		
Other general expenses	4,000	41,000		4,000	40,500	
Total Operating Expenses			132,000			137,000
Income from operations			17,000			24,000
Deduct (Add) financial expenses (revenues):						
Bond interest expense		2,000			2,000	
Interest expense on notes		700			200	
		2,700			2,200	
Interest income		200	2,500		400	1,800
Income on ordinary items (before tax)			14,500			22,200
Less: Applicable income tax expense			7,000			8,200
Income on ordinary items (after applicable tax) . .			7,500			14,000
Extraordinary items:						
Casualty loss*		3,000				
Less: Applicable income tax savings		1.000	2.000			
Net income (after Tax and Extraordinary Items) . .			$ 5,500			$ 14,000

* Assumed to be both unusual and infrequent.

SAMPLE COMPANY, INCORPORATED
Statements of Retained Earnings for the Years Ended December 31, 19B and 19C

	19B		19C	
Retained earnings, balance January 1		$51,500		$53,000
Prior period adjustment:				
Correction of 19A understatement in the				
recorded amount of sales	$5,000			
Less: Tax effect	2,000	3,000		
Retained earnings, balance—adjusted, January 1 . .		54,500		53,000
Add: Net income for the year		5,500		14,000
Total		60,000		67,000
Deductions during the year:				
Dividends on common stock	4,500		$4,500	
Dividends on preferred stock	2,500	7,000	2,500	7,000
Retained Earnings, Balance December 31		$53,000		$60,000

Footnotes

As mentioned above, footnote disclosures are vital for adequate interpretation of financial statements. As further evidence of this point, the following items included in Illustration 4–1 would ordinarily be expected to be more fully explained in footnotes or perhaps in a narrative summary of financial matters pertaining to the financial statements.

Reference	*Nature of the Footnote*
Income Statement:	
Title	Whether financial statements are consolidated or pertain to Sample Company only; principles of consolidation.
Merchandise inventory	Cost flow assumption (Lifo, Fifo, etc.); application of lower of cost or market to inventories.
Depreciation	Method of depreciation; estimated useful lives of depreciable assets.
Interest expense	Interest rates and maturity dates of bonds and notes; any related collateral arrangements; restrictions on dividends.
Income tax expense	*Effective* income tax rate; whether and how income taxes are allocated to periods; manner of accounting for the investment tax credit; presence of tax loss carrybacks and forwards.
Casualty loss	Nature of the loss; insurance recoveries; tax effects.
Retained Earnings Statement:	
Damages paid	Nature of plaintiff's claim.

These are but a few examples of footnote disclosures. Others which are routinely included in financial statements but for which no ready reference exists in Illustration 4–1 are: accounting changes, pension methods and actuarial assumptions, leaseholds, contingent liabilities, subsequent events, translation of foreign currencies, special methods of revenue and expense recognition, amortization period for intangible assets, and many others. Throughout the remainder of this book, references will be made to the need for footnotes. In most cases, they will not be written out due to space limitations. Furthermore, a deeper understanding of footnote disclosures can only be obtained by scrutiny of the footnotes in *actual* published financial statements. These may be obtained from most libraries.

Income Taxes

Reference was made to income tax expenses in the list above. Income taxes present unique accounting problems for a number of reasons, all of which are related to the fact that there are *statutory* tax requirements with which the *financial* accounting system must deal. For example, income tax regulations permit companies that make installment sales to pay income taxes based on cash receipts. This *taxable income* per the income tax return differs from the financial statement income, which equals the installment sales for the period (whether or not collected). Thus, the income tax *liability,* as computed on the tax return, is not equal to the income tax *expense,* as reflected on the income statement, due to timing differences in the recognition of tax and book income. There are a number of other items that give rise to differences in timing of the recognition of revenue and expense for book and tax purposes. All such *timing differences* give rise to the need for interperiod income tax allocation.

In addition to timing differences, there are also certain items which are taxed in a manner that is inconsistent with financial accounting theory. Such items give rise to *permanent differences* in the recognition of revenue and expense for book and tax purposes. Interperiod income tax allocation procedures are *not* appropriate for items of permanent difference. Accounting for income taxes is covered more fully in Chapter 11.

Earnings per Share (EPS)

Earnings per share (EPS) of *common stock* in its simplest form is net income divided by the number of shares of common stock outstanding. The EPS number is accorded special importance in the financial community because a widely quoted statistic, the price-earnings ratio pertaining to a share of stock, has EPS in the denominator. For example, a company whose stock sells for $50 and which earns $4 per share on outstanding common has a price-earnings ratio of 12.5. Complexities (of increasing magnitude) in EPS computations arise when the company—

1. Has preferred stock outstanding.
2. Purchases or issues additional shares of common stock.
3. Has common stock warrants outstanding.
4. Has convertible bonds payable outstanding.

Detailed EPS computations are covered in Chapter 17.

Accounting Changes

One of the principles of accounting is labeled *consistency*. The principle states, in effect, that an entity's results of operations and financial position should be comparable over time. This principle follows from the fact that analysts use interperiod comparisons in time series analyses and other forecasting techniques. When there are structural shifts in an entity's economic base (however measured), however, the entity prior to the shift may be quite different from the entity of the same name subsequent to the shift. In this hypothetical case, the entity may need to make some changes in its accounting methods and/or estimates in order to portray economic reality in its financial statements.

The accounting profession recognizes this as a very real problem. And in an effort to allow a reasonable amount of flexibility to companies in their accounting and financial reporting, the profession allows certain accounting changes to be made. This flexibility can also create problems insofar as companies may use this latitude to manipulate their reported net income. Therefore, to "standardize" the accounting for and reporting of accounting changes, the Accounting Principles Board (APB) in 1971 issued its *Opinion No. 20,* wherein it delineated three distinctly different types of accounting changes and specified the accounting and disclosure requirements for each. The three types of accounting changes involve changes in (*a*) the reporting entity (e.g., from *consolidated* to *separate* financial statements), (*b*) accounting principles (e.g., from one depreciation method to another method), and (*c*) accounting estimates (e.g., of the loss rate on receivables). The accounting for accounting changes is covered in Chapter 20.

Extraordinary, Unusual, and Infrequent Items on the Income Statement (special items of gain and loss)

Prior to 1966 special gain and loss items were reported in a variety of different ways. Some companies reported them on the income statement, similar to the Casualty Loss in Illustration 4–1. Other companies reported special items on the retained earnings statement, effectively *bypassing* the income statement. In order to standardize the reporting of these special items of gain or loss, *APB Opinion No. 9* was issued in 1966. Then in 1973 *APB Opinion No. 30* drew even finer distinctions in reporting special items of income. Currently such items are properly reported on the *income statement* of the period during which they occur (they are not reported on the statement of retained earnings). Furthermore the various subclassifications of special items are distinguished as follows:

1. Extraordinary items—gains and losses that are *both* infrequent and unusual, in relation to the environment in which they occur. For example, hurricane damages along the Gulf Coast would not be *extraordinary,* but a loss due to expropriation of assets in France would be.
2. Unusual items—gains and losses that are *unusual* but which may be expected to recur in the foreseeable future, in relation to the environment in which they occur.
3. Infrequent items—gains and losses that are not unusual but which would *not* be expected to *recur* in the foreseeable future, in relation to the environment in which they occur.

Extraordinary items must be reported separately on the income statement *below* the line "income before extraordinary items." *Unusual* items, as well as *infrequent* items, should also be reported on the income statement covering the period when they occur. Unlike extraordinary items, they must be reported *above* the caption "income before extraordinary items." They should be clearly identified in the body of the income statement as arising from events that are outside the reporting entity's major activities. Many analysts *exclude* these *special gains and losses* for their own predictive purposes because such items reflect on the results of enterprise decisions which are less predictable than the results of the company's ordinary activities.

Prior Period Adjustments

The retained earnings statement in Illustration 4–1 includes only one prior period adjustment, a correction of an understatement in the recorded amount of 19A sales. This error thus caused the 19A ending (19B beginning) balance in the retained earnings account to be understated by the after-tax amount of $3,000. The prior period adjustment corrects this error and places the accounts on a sound footing as of January 1, 19B. However, the prior period adjustment can never alter the fact that the financial statement users had erroneous revenue and income data in 19A. In order to partially compensate for this prior presentation of misinformation for 19A it is common for companies to retroactively restate the financial statements of the affected prior period on the correct basis. For example, if Sample Company's error had been made in 19B, the 19C *reporting* of the prior period adjustment would have entailed a retroactive restatement of 19B sales revenue, income tax expense, and net income on the *correct* basis. In Illustration 4–1, however, the error was made in 19A, and only two years' data (19B and 19C) are presented in comparative form. Therefore, the only appropriate way to report this prior period adjustment is by an adjustment of the January 1, 19B balance in retained earnings.

The fact that prior period adjustments can only correct the effects of misinformation on a retroactive basis suggests that extreme caution be exercised in identifying such items. Therefore, *FASB Statement No. 16* (June 1977) limits prior period adjustments to only two specific items: error corrections and adjustments that result from realization of income tax benefits of pre-acquisition operating loss carryforwards of purchased subsidiaries. All other items of revenue, expense, gain, and loss must be reported, at the time they are realized, on the income statement for that particular period.

The Retained Earnings Statement

In general, the statement of retained earnings reports the period's reconciliation between beginning and ending retained earnings. Primary among the reconciling items are (*a*) net income and (*b*) dividends. Rarely will a company report a prior period adjustment; however, if appropriate it should appear on this statement. Certain treasury stock transactions also may directly affect the retained earnings account, in which case they too will be reported here. Chapters 16 and 17 give special consideration to the Retained Earnings account.

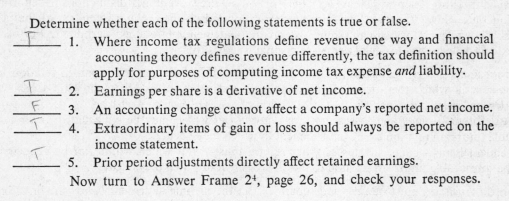

Determine whether each of the following statements is true or false.

___I___ 1. Where income tax regulations define revenue one way and financial accounting theory defines revenue differently, the tax definition should apply for purposes of computing income tax expense *and* liability.

___T___ 2. Earnings per share is a derivative of net income.

___F___ 3. An accounting change cannot affect a company's reported net income.

___T___ 4. Extraordinary items of gain or loss should always be reported on the income statement.

___T___ 5. Prior period adjustments directly affect retained earnings.

Now turn to Answer Frame 2⁴, page 26, and check your responses.

chapter 5

REVIEW—THE BALANCE SHEET AND THE STATEMENT OF CHANGES IN FINANCIAL POSITION

This chapter is divided into two parts. Frame 1[5] covers the balance sheet, and Frame 2[5] covers the statement of changes in financial position.

Frame 1[5]

The Balance Sheet

This is the "position statement"; that is, it presents the financial position of a firm at a specific point in time. The balance sheet is always dated "at" or "as of" a certain date; for example, "Statement of Assets, Liabilities, and Owners' Equity (a preferable title) at December 31, 19A." The balance sheet reports on the financial position of the business at a specific date in terms of the financial position model: Assets = Liabilities + Owners' Equity. The balance sheet classifications will be reviewed in the paragraphs to follow. Although there is some variation to be found in practice in balance sheet structure (arrangement and terminology), the following classifications are representative of current accounting practice:

Assets	*Liabilities*
1. Current assets.	1. Current liabilities.
2. Investments and funds.	2. Long-term liabilities.
3. Operational (fixed) assets—tangible.	*Stockholders' Equity*
4. Operational (fixed) assets—intangible.	1. Contributed capital:
5. Other assets.	*a.* Capital stock.
6. Deferred charges.	*b.* Contributed capital in excess of par or stated values.
	2. Retained earnings:
	a. Appropriated.
	b. Unappropriated.
	3. Unrealized capital.

Current Assets. This category includes cash and other assets and resources reasonably expected to be realized in cash or sold or consumed within one year, or during the normal *operating cycle* of the business, whichever is longer. Current assets should be listed on the balance sheet in order of their liquidity. The

Answer frame 2⁴

1. True. An example is interest revenue earned on bonds that the U.S. Constitution precludes the federal government from taxing. Such interest is *tax-free*. Therefore, a company should not compute any tax on this revenue, although from an accounting standpoint the revenue has the same (positive) effect on owners' equity as taxable revenue.
2. True. EPS can be an exceedingly complex computation, but it is based on net income (and the number of shares of common stock outstanding).
3. False. A change in inventory method, for example, can have a substantial effect on net income. Many other accounting changes also have *some* effect on net income.
4. True. They are required to be shown on the income statement.
5. True. But, if, for example, a prior period adjustment pertains to 19A and is corrected in 19B, the company may choose in 19B to *restate* the 19A income statement to include the item—for purposes of comparatively reporting 19A's income statement along with the 19B income statement.

If you missed any of the above questions, you should reread Frame 2⁴ before proceeding.

You have now completed the review of the income statement. Continue reading with Chapter 5, a similar review of the balance sheet and the statement of changes in financial position.

Frame 1⁵ continued

operating cycle of the business is defined as the period of time between the acquisition of inventory (for sale) or items which will be processed to become salable inventory, and the final cash realization from their sale; the operating cycle is cash, to inventory, to sales, to receivables, and back to cash. *Working capital* is defined as current assets minus current liabilities.

Investments and Funds.   *Long-term* investments and funds (cash, invested or otherwise) set aside for nonworking capital purposes constitute the two items reported under this balance sheet classification. *Short-term* investments are current assets, and as such are not classified as "Investments."

Operational Assets.   Those assets which a business more or less permanently retains, not for sale but rather for use in its operations, are defined as operational (or fixed) assets. They are classified as *tangible* when they have physical characteristics, such as land, buildings, machinery, furniture, fixtures, and natural resources. Those having a limited life are subject to depreciation and depletion. Operational assets are classified as *intangible* when they have no physical form (though they may be evidenced by various tangible documents) and when their value is the rights or benefits their possession confers upon the owner; examples are patents, copyrights, goodwill, trademarks, brand names, leaseholds, formulas, franchises, organization costs, and special rights (such as mineral or water). Intangible fixed assets have a limited life and are subject to periodic amortization.

Other Assets.   This is a miscellaneous category sometimes used for items which cannot be realistically listed under the other classifications; included are such items as fixed assets not being used but held for resale. This classification should be used only when essential.

Deferred Charges.   Occasionally, a balance sheet will also report a classification entitled "deferred charges." Deferred charges are similar to prepaid expenses in that they represent debit balances derived from expenditures which presumably will benefit a number of future periods. Deferred charges are distinguished from prepaid expenses on the basis of the time over which they will be amortized; that is, the amortization involves a longer period of time than for prepaid expenses; the latter must agree with the definition of current assets given above. Sometimes deferred charges are reported as other assets.

Current Liabilities.   This category includes those liabilities which are expected to be paid with funds (resources) listed on the same balance sheet as current assets (or through the creation of other current liabilities). Typical current liabilities are accounts and notes payable, accrued expenses, taxes payable, unearned (prepaid) income, advances from customers, and cash dividends payable. Current maturities of long-term notes, bonds, and mortgages should also be included in this category.

Long-Term Liabilities. All liabilities not properly classified as current liabilities should be reported under this caption. Examples are bonds payable, long-term notes payable, and mortgages payable.

Capital Stock. The par value or stated value (or other appropriate amount in the case of nopar stock) of the total number of shares of stock *issued* should be reported for each class of stock along with the number of shares authorized, issued, and subscribed, and other relevant features. Account titles reflecting positive (credit) balances include Preferred Stock, Common Stock, and Subscribed Stock; an account title with a contra (debit) balance is Treasury Stock.

Contributed Capital in Excess of Par or Stated Value. This category includes premium on capital stock and other values received from shareholders above par or stated values. Another, but less desirable title is "additional paid-in capital."

Retained Earnings. This classification consists of the accumulation of net income less distributions to shareholders (cash and stock dividends). It involves two subcategories: (1) unappropriated retained earnings and (2) appropriated retained earnings. The latter represents restrictions on retained earnings as a result of (1) legal requirements, (2) contractual requirements, or (3) managerial discretion. Typical accounts in appropriated retained earnings are: Reserve for Bond Sinking Fund, Retained Earnings Set Aside for Future Plant Expansion, and Reserve for Expected Future Inventory Price Declines.

Unrealized Capital. This classification accommodates the write-down of long-term investments to a market value below cost, which represents a negative (or debit) balance in the Unrealized Capital account. This particular usage of the Unrealized Capital account became common in 1975, when FASB *Statement No. 12* began requiring companies to account for certain long-term investments in stock on a lower-of-cost-or-market basis. Other types of *unrealized capital* are rare.

Concepts of Valuation

Chapter 4 discussed different concepts of income. Income measurement can be viewed as one side of a coin, and asset valuation as the other side. Frequent references were made to the *historical-cost* model of accounting. Those earlier references, in the context of the income statement, refer to the fact that *historical costs* are matched against revenues in arriving at net income. This implies with equal force that, in general, assets are valued at historical cost. However, conservatism sometimes dictates the write-down of an asset to a current value below cost to reflect the impairment of an asset value.

In the future, this argument may be extended to imply that *if* the current replacement cost of expired assets (expenses) were to be matched against current revenue, then the unexpired assets would also be valued at the current cost of replacing them. This hypothetical write-up would occasion the recognition of *holding gains* (so long as current replacement cost exceeds historical cost), which the historical-cost accounting model ignores.

Other accountants favor valuing assets at the present value of future cash flows or current market values (i.e., selling prices) on the theory that business activity places all assets in a perpetual state of liquidation. In this view, the current market value of an asset is the best measure of the value of the asset to the enterprise. There is little doubt that users of financial statements would like to have *objective* market value data on the entity's assets and liabilities; however, the usefulness of some market value data is seriously limited because of the inherent subjectivity of "value" measures (except, of course, those evidenced by completed transactions). For this reason market value accounting has gained acceptability for only a limited class of balance sheet items, namely investments in stock (for which objective data are available) held by financial institutions whose major activity is making such investments.

Importance of the Balance Sheet

The balance sheet, or position statement, is viewed by some as being somewhat less important than the income statement—due to the overriding importance of the net income number on the income state-

Illustration 5–1

SAMPLE COMPANY, INCORPORATED
Balance Sheets at December 31, 19B and 19C

	19B		19C	
Assets				
Current Assets:				
Cash		$ 51,000		$ 57,500
Notes receivable (contingent liability from notes discounted $3,000)		5,000		5,000
Accounts receivable	$ 34,000		$ 36,500	
Less: Allowance for doubtful accounts	2,000	32,000	2,000	34,500
Merchandise inventory		90,000		82,000
Prepaid expenses		1,000		1,500
Total Current Assets		179,000		180,500
Investments and Funds:				
Bond sinking fund		30,000		33,000
Tangible Fixed Assets:				
Store equipment	105,000		110,000	
Less: Accumulated depreciation	40,000	65,000	42,000	68,000
Intangible Fixed Assets:				
Patent (cost less amortization)		8,000		7,000
Other Assets:				
Obsolete equipment held for resale (estimated net realizable value)		1,000		1,000
Total Assets		$283,000		$289,500
Liabilities				
Current Liabilities:				
Accounts payable		$ 59,000		$ 60,000
Notes payable, short term		9,000		10,000
Wages payable		22,000		11,500
Income tax payable		2,000		4,500
Total Current Liabilities		92,000		86,000
Long-Term Liabilities:				
Notes payable, long term		2,000		
Bonds payable		50,000		55,000
Total Liabilities		144,000		141,000
Stockholders' Equity				
Contributed Capital:				
Capital Stock:				
Preferred stock, par $50, authorized and outstanding 500 shares	25,000		25,000	
Common stock, par $10, authorized shares, 10,000; issued and outstanding, 5,200 shares at December 31, 19B, and 5,400 shares at December 31, 19C	52,000		54,000	
Total Capital Stock	77,000		79,000	
Contributed Capital in Excess of Par Value:				
On preferred stock $4,000		$4,000		
On common stock 5,000	9,000	5,500	9,500	
Total Contributed Capital	86,000		88,500	
Retained Earnings (see statement of retained earnings Chapter 4)	53,000		60,000	
Total Stockholders' Equity		139,000		148,500
Total Liabilities and Stockholders' Equity		$283,000		$289,500

ment. But the balance sheet serves a vital informational role in presenting the financial position of the entity (which of course includes a listing of the liabilities) at a point in time. Unlike the income statement, no single balance sheet item dominates its usefulness. For example, *working capital* ratios are useful in predicting the ability to pay short-term debts, the *ratio of liabilities to owners' equity* is used for assessing long-run financial stability, and the composition of individual assets and liabilities constitutes important information. Furthermore, certain meaningful relationships combine one or more income statement items with one or more balance sheet items for financial analysis. Chapter 23 covers that material in some detail.

Illustration 5–1 above presents reasonably detailed balance sheets for two years.

Footnotes

It is necessary to disclose important accounting information that would be cumbersome to report on the face of the balance sheet. The student should refer once again to the representative list of footnotes given in Chapter 4. Virtually every one of the footnotes listed would relate to the three separate financial statements. For example, in Illustration 5–1 above, the "Merchandise Inventory" footnote would disclose the cost flow assumption (Lifo, Fifo, etc.) used to compute inventory cost. This added information illuminates the balance sheet valuation of the asset (inventory) as well as the related income statement expense (cost of goods sold). Thus, one should recognize that (1) footnotes are necessary and (2) the same set of footnotes often yields income statement, balance sheet, and statement of changes in financial position information.

True or false?

_____ T _ 1.   The truth of the financial position model: Assets = Liabilities + Owners' Equity *always* holds.

_____ F _ 2.   If a company has *beginning* assets of $2,000 and liabilities of $1,500, earns net income of $600, pays dividends of $200, and has ending liabilities of $1,500, its ending assets total $2,000.

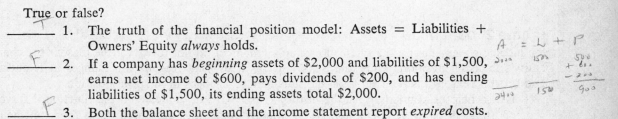

_____ F _ 3.   Both the balance sheet and the income statement report *expired* costs.

_____ F _ 4.   Different valuation models (historical cost, current replacement cost, current market value) would report essentially the same amount of owners' equity for a company. Only the amounts reported for assets and liabilities would differ.

Now gauge your understanding by comparing your responses with those given in Answer Frame 1[5], page 30.

Frame 2[5]

The Statement of Changes in Financial Position (SCFP)

The third primary financial statement, the SCFP, has been required only since 1971 when the APB issued *Opinion No. 19* entitled "Reporting Changes in Financial Position." Prior to that time presentation of this data in published financial reports was optional, although many companies voluntarily presented *funds flow* data similar to the type that now appears in the SCFP.

To put the SCFP in perspective it is necessary to return to Frame 1[4] of Chapter 4. Note in the diagram that the SCFP constitutes one of the "bridges" between successive balance sheets. Also recall that the balance sheets are *statements of financial position* and that the income statement and retained earnings statement include information regarding *changes in financial position*. The important point is that

Answer frame 1[5]

1. True. Accounting error may cause the *recorded* amount of the assets not to equal the sum of the records of the amount of liabilities and owners' equities, but the underlying relationship *always* holds nevertheless.
2. False. Ending assets must total $2,400, computed as follows:

	Assets	= Liabilities	+ Owners' Equity	
Beginning . . .	$2,000	$1,500	$ 500	(computed from
Net income . . .			600	Assets − Liabilities)
Dividends . . .			(200)	
	$2,400	= $1,500 (given) +	$ 900	

Note that we could not be sure of the specific effects that transactions giving rise to net income of $600 had on assets and liabilities. But if we know (can compute) ending owners' equity and ending liabilities, we can compute ending assets. Thus, we can *summarize* the changes in assets, liabilities, and owners' equity even if we cannot infer all the transactions.

3. False. The balance sheet reports *unexpired* costs for assets.
4. False. Different amounts for assets and liabilities would imply different amounts for owners' equity—based on the financial position model. The only exception would be identically offsetting differences in assets and liabilities; in this case, owners' equity would be unaffected.

If you missed any of the above, reread Frame 1[5] before beginning Frame 2[5], page 29.

Frame 2[5] continued

the income statement and the retained earnings statement do not reveal *all* the reasons for changes in the entity's financial position. Thus, the SCFP reveals additional reasons for changes in financial position, and for this reason it is referred to as the statement of changes in financial position.

It is also helpful to briefly trace the history of the SCFP to understand the function it serves in financial reporting. Prior to *APB Opinion No. 19,* many companies presented funds flow statements that accounted for the changes in "funds" during the interval between two balance sheets. "Funds" were variously defined as (*a*) *cash* or (*b*) *cash and near-cash assets* or (*c*) *working capital* (current assets minus current liabilities) depending on the company's preference. Thus the funds statement reported the reasons for changes in, for example, working capital, ignoring business transactions that had no direct effect on working capital. This omission left some very important financing and investing activities of the enterprise completely unreported in the financial statements. *APB Opinion No. 19* remedied this omission by requiring that *all* financing and investing activities be reported on the SCFP. An example of a formerly omitted transaction would be the purchase of operational assets (such as land and buildings) with long-term debt.

Concepts of Reporting Changes in Financial Position

The discussion above states that older "funds" statements were prepared on one of three bases: (*a*) cash, (*b*) cash and near-cash assets, or (*c*) working capital. The same is true of present-day SCFPs, but the SCFP also contains a section for financing and investing activities not affecting cash (*or* cash and near-cash *or* working capital). And companies still may choose among these bases on which to prepare the SCFP. The authors prefer cash (or cash plus near cash) as the underlying basis because of (1) the difficulty in manipulating cash and (2) the more basic nature of cash (vis-à-vis working capital, which is a residual). But whatever basis the company uses, it is compelled to also report its other financial position changes that do not directly affect that basis.

Importance of the SCFP

Most financial observers agree that the SCFP is important; however, it is difficult to ascertain exactly *how important* it is, perhaps because it is relatively new. It seems fair to conclude that it is, in general, somewhat less important in financial analysis than the income statement or the balance sheet. When directly queried on this point, respondents often reply that the information presented in the SCFP is used to amplify or clarify specific items presented on the other two financial statements, where those other disclosures standing alone are not altogether clear. Also, some analysts use the SCFP on an "exception" basis, that is, to highlight particularly favorable or unfavorable factors.

At the opposite extreme are those who view the SCFP as the *most important* financial statement, due largely to deficiencies in the other two primary financial statements. This last group appreciates the fact that the SCFP is essentially a cash-basis income statement. Therefore, to the extent that it presents cash flows, in addition to the accrual basis net income that is reported on the income statement, the SCFP presents additional information, which many find helpful.

Illustration 5–2 below presents the format of the SCFP—prepared on the cash basis. Note that there are three major sections of the statement, outlined as follows:

1. Sources of cash.
    a. From operations (income statement sources).
    b. From other sources.
2. Uses of cash (from other than operations).
3. Financing and investing activities not affecting cash.

Also note that the 19C statement of changes in financial position presented in Illustration 5–2 articulates with the balance sheet presented in Illustration 5–1 and with the income statement and the statement of

Illustration 5–2

SAMPLE CORPORATION, INCORPORATED
Statement of Changes in Financial Position—Cash Basis
For the Year Ended December 31, 19C

Sources of Cash:		
From operations:		
Net income (accrual basis) before extraordinary loss		$14,000
Add noncash expenses and add or deduct other adjustments to derive cash basis:		
Depreciation and amortization expenses	$ 3,000	
Increase in trade accounts receivable	(2,500)	
Decrease in merchandise inventory	8,000	
Increase in prepaid expenses	(500)	
Decrease in current liabilities	(6,000)	2,000
Total cash generated by operations, exclusive of extraordinary loss .		16,000
Extraordinary items—none		–0–
Total Cash Generated by Operations		16,000
From other sources:		
Issued common stock for cash		2,500
Total Sources of Cash during the Year		18,500
Uses of Cash:		
Dividends paid in cash	7,000	
Paid into bond sinking fund	3,000	
Paid off long-term note payable prior to maturity	2,000	
Total Uses of Cash during the Year		12,000
Net Increase in Cash during the Year		$ 6,500
Financing and Investing Activities Not Affecting Cash during the Year:		
Issued bonds payable to acquire store equipment		$ 5,000

retained earnings presented in Illustration 4–1. Thus taken together these financial statements constitute an example of a *complete* set of financial statements (excluding the footnotes).

Preparation of the SCFP requires some facility with the accounts that can be explained more efficiently after more experience is gained. For this reason, the mechanical aspects of preparing the statement are deferred until Chapter 21. The interested reader can go directly to that chapter for detailed coverage of the SCFP.

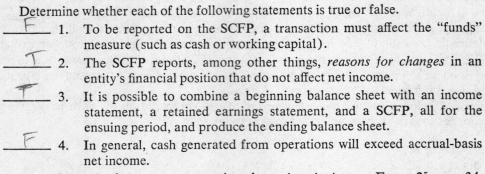

Determine whether each of the following statements is true or false.

____F____ 1. To be reported on the SCFP, a transaction must affect the "funds" measure (such as cash or working capital).

____T____ 2. The SCFP reports, among other things, *reasons for changes* in an entity's financial position that do not affect net income.

____T____ 3. It is possible to combine a beginning balance sheet with an income statement, a retained earnings statement, and a SCFP, all for the ensuing period, and produce the ending balance sheet.

____F____ 4. In general, cash generated from operations will exceed accrual-basis net income.

Now check your answers against those given in Answer Frame 2⁵, page 34.

chapter 6

CONCEPTS OF FUTURE AND PRESENT VALUE

Frame 1[6]

Concepts of future and present value (often referred to simply as *present value*) are rooted in the time value of money. That is, a person who is given a choice between receipt of a sum of money now *or* at some future time should choose immediate receipt because it can be invested now to earn a return over the future period. If the later receipt is chosen, the return is foregone.

Present value concepts are applied in a wide variety of business applications. Examples are capital budgeting, bond valuation, leases, pensions, discounting receivables and payables, and fund accumulations. Therefore, a firm grasp of this material is essential. It is fortunate that most of the applications utilize one or more or *four* key concepts, viz:

1. Future amount of 1.
2. Present value of 1.
3. Future amount of annuity of 1.
4. Present value of annuity of 1.

The remainder of this chapter is divided into four parts: this frame covers future amount of 1 and present value of 1; Frame 2[6] covers the future amount of annuity of 1; Frame 3[6] covers the present value of annuity of 1; and Frame 4[6] covers several complications in present value problems.

Future Amount of 1 (FA of 1)[1]

FA of 1 refers specifically to the future amount of $1 (*now*) taken to the end of *n* periods at a compound interest rate, *i*. The formula is given by Equation 1:

$$\text{FA of } 1 = (1 + i)^n \quad \text{(see Table 6–1 at the end of this chapter)} \tag{1}$$

Example 1: If $10,000 is paid into a fund that could be invested to earn 8% per period for three periods, the *future amount* of the fund at the end of the third period is equal to $12,597 ($10,000 × FA of 1 at 8% for 3 periods = $10,000 × 1.25971—from Table 6–1).

---

[1] Future "amount" and present "value" are labels the authors find helpful in distinguishing the two concepts; the reader will encounter other labels as well.

Answer frame 2⁵

1. False. Note in Illustration 5–2 that the final section reports financing and investing activities that do *not* affect the "funds" measure. Therefore, the SCFP reports *all* financing and investing activities.
2. True. Note in Illustration 5–2 the "other" source of cash, from issuing common stock. That transaction did not affect net income, but it did affect the cash (or financial) position of the Sample Company.
3. True. This is implied by the title, the statement of *changes* in financial position. Therefore, if beginning financial position and the changes in financial position for a period are known, then ending financial position can be computed. In most cases, the income statement and the retained earnings statement are also needed because they often contain data on financial position changes that cannot be extracted from the SCFP.
4. True or false. There is no general answer to this question. Refer to Illustration 5–2. If we were to change *any one* of the components of "cash generated by operations," the cash generated would also be affected. Therefore, the answer is situation specific.

If you missed any of the above, reread Frame 2⁵ before beginning Chapter 6.

Frame 1⁶ continued

Present Value of 1 (PV of 1)

PV of 1 refers specifically to the present value (*now*) of $1 to be paid or received at the end of n future periods, discounted to a present value at a compound interest rate, i. Thus present value is less than future amount. The formula is given by Equation 2:

$$\text{PV of } 1 = \frac{1}{(1 + i)^n} \quad \text{(see Table 6–2 at the end of this chapter)} \tag{2}$$

Example 2: If you negotiate the total price of $12,597 (including interest) for a machine and the seller agrees to let you pay the $12,597 at the end of three years, with a compound interest rate of 8% per period, the cost of the machine (measured as the *present value* of the debt) is $10,000 ($12,597 × PV of 1 at 8% for 3 periods = $12,597 × .79383—from Table 6–2).

In summary, both FA of 1 and PV of 1 refer uniquely to *lump (or single) sums,* as opposed to a stream of equal periodic amounts, which constitutes an annuity.

Now check your progress by answering each of the following questions.

_____ 1. In absolute dollar amounts, the present value of 1 always exceeds the future amount of 1 because of the interest that can be earned on the present value.

_____ 2. Present value of 1 is equal to the reciprocal of future amount of 1.

_____ 3. Future amount problems can be solved as present value problems, and present value problems can be solved as future amount problems.

_____ 4. The concept of compound interest means that interest is paid on interest (earned in prior periods) as well as on principal.

Compare your responses to those given in Answer Frame 1⁶, page 36.

Frame 2[6]

The term "annuity" refers to a series of equal amounts paid or received at specified periodic intervals. Note that the concept of an annuity is general in that the term annuity is *used to refer* to equal amounts paid or received at *equal* intervals that are *not necessarily annual* intervals. The equal periodic amounts paid or received are called *rents*. Annuity problems are thus distinguished from future amount of 1 and present value of 1 (covered in Frame 1[6]) because the latter two involve a single lump sum rather than a stream of periodic rents.

Annuity problems can be rather complex. For this reason it is advisable to diagram annuity problems in terms of the number of (*a*) rents and (*b*) periods involved (note that an annuity involves one rent for each period). Once the problems are correctly diagrammed, they can generally be solved straightforwardly; thus the diagram is crucially important.

Future Amount of Annuity

Definition: The FA of an ordinary annuity is the *future* (accumulated) amount of a series of rents (*R*) at the compound interest rate (*i*), on the date of the last rent.

Implicit in the definition given above is the fact that the annuity is an *end-of-the-period* concept (generally called an ordinary annuity). Or, in diagrammatic form, the definition of the FA of an annuity of six rents appears as:

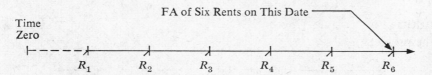

In a sense, the first period (represented in the diagram by the dotted line) has little meaning since the first rent occurs at the end of this period. Therefore, no interest accumulates during this first period. Note that, in accordance with the definition of FA, the above diagram reflects:

a. Six equal rents.
b. Six equal periods, and
c. That the sixth rent, which occurs on the last day of the final interest period, earns *no* interest (thus, there is interest for only five periods).

The formula for the future amount of an annuity of *n* rents (*R*) at the interest rate *i* is given by Equation 3:

$$\text{FA of } n \text{ rents of 1 each at } i = \frac{(1+i)^n - 1}{i} \text{ (see Table 6-3)} \tag{3}$$

Table 6-3 provides the FA of *n* rents of one each at *i* *as of* the date of the last rent (R_6) in the diagram above (i.e., the table shows ordinary annuity values).

Example 3:   Assume that you decide to invest $2,000 at the end of each of seven years in a college education fund for your daughter. The first investment will be made on her 12th birthday (end of Year 1) and the last investment on her 18th birthday (i.e., 7 rents). The investment will earn 7% per year, and the entire accumulation may be withdrawn by her on her 18th birthday. How much will she have for college on her 18th birthday?

The answer is $17,308, computed as follows:

Answer frame 1⁶

1. False. In absolute terms, FA of 1 exceeds PV of 1 by the amount of the interest that is *included in* the future amount and not included in the present value.
2. True. This is clear from the formulas given in Equations 1 and 2.
3. True. This follows directly from the reciprocal relationship between FA and PV. More specifically,

$$\text{FA of any amount} = \text{PV of the same amount} \times (1 + i)^n$$

and

$$\text{PV of any amount} = \text{FA of the same amount} \times \frac{1}{(1 + i)^n}$$

These, of course, are simply restatements of the basic formulas.

4. True. For example, $100 invested at 9% for two years is computed as follows:

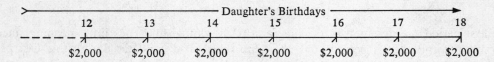

Note that in Year 2, the total interest of $9.81 is comprised of interest of $9 on the original investment plus $.81 of interest on the first year interest of $9.

If you missed any of the above, reread Frame 1⁶ before beginning Frame 2⁶, page 35.

Frame 2⁶ continued

Step 1—Diagram the problem.

```
                        ──────── Daughter's Birthdays ────────▶
         12        13        14        15        16        17        18
─ ─ ─ ─ ─┼─────────┼─────────┼─────────┼─────────┼─────────┼─────────┼
       $2,000    $2,000    $2,000    $2,000    $2,000    $2,000    $2,000
```

On 18th birthday, what will be the total dollars in the fund?

[Note in the diagram that it is an end-of-the-period (i.e., ordinary) annuity.]

Step 2—Write the equation to define the problem.

FA of 7 rents of $2,000 each at 7% = $2,000 × FA of 7 rents of 1 each at 7%

Step 3—Identify known and unknown values; then insert the known values in the above equation and solve for the unknown. The amount of each rent ($2,000) is known, and the FA of seven rents of one each can be obtained from Table 6–3. Therefore,

FA of 7 rents of $2,000 each at 7% = $2,000 × 8.65402 (from Table 6–3)
= $17,308 (i.e., the fund accumulation on daughter's 18th birthday)

Modifications of the Future Amount of Annuity (annuity due)

We could have written the problem situation in Example 3 above to have asked, "How much cash would the daughter have in the education fund on the day immediately preceding her 19th birthday,[2]

―――――――――

[2] This particular situation, viz, the FA of an annuity *one period after the date of the last rent*, is referred to as the FA of an annuity *due*.

with all other facts held constant?" Since interest for one more year would accumulate (but not one more rent), this (new) problem can be solved by slightly modifying the solution to the problem given in Example 3. The solution to this (new) problem proceeds as follows:

1. The future accumulated amount of 7 rents as of the daughter's 18th birthday is $17,308, as given above.
2. The future accumulated amount of 7 rents, *one year later* (just before her 19th birthday), is equal to the FA of 7 rents (computed above) multiplied by 1.07 (or, $18,520) to give effect to the facts that:
    a. There is *no* additional rent on her 19th birthday (the rents stop on her 18th birthday), and
    b. The accumulated amount as of her 18th birthday continues to earn interest *at 7% per year* until the day preceding her 19th birthday.

   Note that this modified annuity concept in effect is a beginning of the period concept (for each rent) because the accumulation is computed as of the end of the period after the last rent. It is generally referred to as an annuity due (in contrast to an ordinary annuity which as explained and illustrated above is an end-of-the-period concept since the accumulation value is made as of the date of the last rent).

   True or false?

   _____ 1. The FA of 1 for *n* periods is fundamentally the same concept as the FA of an annuity of *n* rents.

   _____ 2. The FA of three annual rents of $20 each at 7% per annum is equal to $64.30.

   _____ 3. The FA of three annual rents of $20 each at 7% per annum, as of the day three years after the date of the last rent is $78.77.

   _____ 4. The time period of the FA of ordinary annuities always ends on the date of the last rent.

   _____ 5. Rents must be paid at annual intervals.

   Now compare your answers with those given in Answer Frame 2[6], page 38.

Frame 3[6]

Present Value of Annuity

Definition: The PV of an annuity is the *present (discounted) value* of a series of rents (R) to be paid or received at equal intervals of time at the compound interest rate (i) at the beginning of the period in which the first rent occurs.

   This definition explicitly recognizes an *end-of-the-period* concept. In diagrammatic form, the definition of PV of an annuity of six end-of-the-period rents appears as:

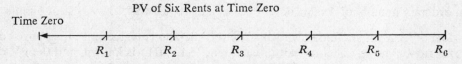

   This end-of-the-period concept of the present value of an annuity is generally called an ordinary annuity.

   The diagram for the PV of an annuity is almost identical to the diagram for the FA of an annuity.

Answer frame 2⁶

1. False. FA of 1 involves the future accumulated amount of a *lump sum*. FA of an annuity involves the future accumulated amount of a *stream of rents*.
2. True. Computations:

$$\$20 \times 3.2149 \text{ (from Table 6–3)} = \$64.30$$

3. True. Computations:

$$\$64.30 \text{ (from Question 2)} \times (1.07)^3 =$$
$$\$64.30 \times 1.22504 \text{ (from Table 6–1)} = \$78.77$$

4. True. This is true by the definition of the FA of an ordinary annuity.
5. False. Rents can be paid at any pre-specified equal interval.

If you missed any of the above, reread Frame 2⁶ before beginning Frame 3⁶, page 37.

Frame 3⁶ continued

The important difference is that the two time lines point in *opposite* directions because one concept focuses on *future* amount while the other concept focuses on *present* value.

The formula for the present value of an ordinary annuity of *n* rents at the interest rate *i* is given by Equation 4:

$$\text{PV of } n \text{ rents of 1 each at } i = \frac{1 - \dfrac{1}{(1+i)^n}}{i} \text{ (see Table 6–4)} \qquad (4)$$

Table 6–4 provides the PV of an ordinary annuity of *n* rents of one each at *i* *as of* time zero in the diagram above.

Example 4:   A new machine is estimated to increase your company's income by $4,000 per year over its six-year estimated life (no residual value). The company requires a 10% annual rate of return on investments of this type. Assume that income is earned at the end of each period. What is the maximum amount you should pay *now* for the machine?
The answer is $17,421, computed as follows:

Step 1—Diagram the problem.

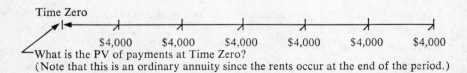

Time Zero

$4,000 $4,000 $4,000 $4,000 $4,000 $4,000

What is the PV of payments at Time Zero?
(Note that this is an ordinary annuity since the rents occur at the end of the period.)

Step 2—Write the equation to define the problem.

PV of an ordinary annuity of 6 rents of $4,000 each at 10% = $4,000 × PV of 6 rents of 1 each at 10%

Step 3—Identify known and unknown values, insert the known values into the above equation, and solve for the unknown. The amount of each rent ($4,000)) is known, and the PV of six rents of one each can be obtained from Table 6–4.

PV of 6 rents of $4,000 each at 10% (i.e., the maximum to be paid for the machine)
= $4,000 × 4.35526 (from Table 6–4) = $17,421

Modifications of the Present Value of Annuity (annuity due)

The problem situation of Example 4 could have been modified to include a down payment of $6,000, with all other factors held constant. In this case, the cost of the machine would be $23,421 ($17,421— from above + $6,000). Or the seller of the machine could have set the down payment at $4,000, which is equal to the amount of each rent. In this case, the cost of the machine would be $21,421 ($17,421 + $4,000). In both of these modified cases (as in the original case that involved no down payment), the cost of the machine is equal to the *present value* of the cash flows required to purchase the machine. In both modified cases the down payment is added (at face value) to the PV of the annuity because the down payment is already stated at present value.

Implicit in this latter modification is that the rents occur at the beginning of the period. That is a beginning-of-the-period concept which is usually referred to as an annuity due. Note that in this assumption the first rent (the $4,000 down payment) is accorded no discounting.

Another modification could be the inclusion of an expected residual value of $2,000 for the machine, with all other factors unchanged in Example 4. In this case, the prospective purchaser would be willing to pay for the machine the sum of:

a. The present value of the stream of expected annual earnings of $4,000 each that the machine can be used to generate, and

b. The present value of the expected (lump-sum) residual value of $2,000 that the machine can be sold for at the end of its six-year life.

Thus this modified problem includes:

a. The present value of an annuity concept, and

b. The present value of 1 concept.

The solution would proceed as follows:

Step 1—Diagram the problem. We already know the present value of the annuity—$17,421—from above. Therefore the following diagram only applies to the PV of the residual value. Note that *no rents* appear in this diagram.

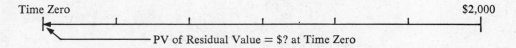

Time Zero $2,000

PV of Residual Value = $? at Time Zero

Step 2—Write the equation to define the problem.

Maximum to be paid for machine = PV of annuity + PV of residual value

Maximum = PV of annuity + ($2,000 × PV of 1 at 10% for 6 periods)

Step 3—Identify the known and unknown values, insert the known values in the above equation, and solve for the unknown. In this problem all values are known, except for the maximum the company is willing to pay.

Maximum = $17,421 + $2,000 × .56447 (from Table 6–2)
= $18,550

Determine whether each of the following questions is true or false.

——— 1. Assets can be appropriately priced at the FA of cash flows necessary to pay for the asset.

——— 2. The PV of an annuity due is a beginning-of-the-period concept, whereas the PV of an ordinary annuity is an end-of-the-period concept.

——— 3. The owner of a machine prices the machine for sale as follows: Pay $1,500 down and $1,000 (which includes interest at 9% per year) at the end of each of the next three years. The purchaser who buys the machine on these terms should record the asset at *cost* of $4,031.

——— 4. Refer once again to the fact situation in Question 3. Keep all factors constant *except* (*a*) the interest rate, which is now 10% per year, and (*b*) the three $1,000 payments are made at the end of six-month periods. The cost of the machine on these terms is also $4,031.

Now refer to Answer Frame 3⁶, page 42.

Frame 4⁶

Complications in Annuity Problems

1. Converison of Stated Interest Rate to Effective Interest Rate. In most of the examples of annuity problems covered thus far in the chapter, the interest was compounded *annually* and the rents also occurred *annually*. If in Example 3 above (the FA of annuity), the savings institution had compounded interest quarterly, the *effective* annual interest rate would have been greater than the stated annual rate of 7%. For cases in which compounding periods occur more frequently than the rents occur, it is necessary to convert the stated rate to the effective rate. This is accomplished by using the following formula:

$$EI = \left(1 + \frac{SI}{C}\right)^{c} - 1$$

where: EI = effective interest rate per rent interval.
SI = stated interest rate per rent interval.
C = number of compounding periods per rent interval.

Using the data in Example 3 above but modified to include quarterly compounding of interest, the effective interest rate is 7.186% per year $\left[\left(1 + \frac{.07}{4}\right)^{4} - 1\right]$. After obtaining this *effective* interest rate *i*, simply use this new *i* in the steps 1–3 given above. This same process would be followed for PV of annuity problems as well—where the compounding periods occur more often than the rents occur. In Example 3, the effective rate would have been 7.123% if interest had been compounded semiannually $\left[\left(1 + \frac{.07}{2}\right)^{2} - 1\right]$.

The formula given above is general in that it also applies to cases in which the rents occur more frequently than the compounding periods. For example, assume that the *annual* compound interest rate is 7% and that rents occur semiannually. In some cases it *may not* be appropriate to divide the 7% annual compound rate into semiannual portions of 3½% each and then to use the 3½% rate in subsequent computations. This treatment is tantamount to changing the annual compound interest rate to 7.123% $[(1.035)^{2} - 1]$. In this case it may be necessary to apply the formula given above to compute the effective semiannual interest rate as $3.441\% \left[\left(1 + \dfrac{.035}{.5}\right)^{.5} - 1, \text{ or } \sqrt[2]{1.07} - 1 \right]$. In most cases, however, it is understood that it *is* acceptable to divide an annual compound rate into periodic portions by simply multiplying the annual rate by the fraction for the periodic segment (e.g., $7\% \times \frac{1}{2} = 3\frac{1}{2}\%$) to compute the interest rate applicable to each semiannual rent period. But the contract will specify which of the two methods of determining the effective semiannual (or other interim period) rate is appropriate.

Since tables do not include interest rates such as 7.186% and 3.441%, it is necessary to use the formulas to solve problems that incorporate such interest rates. In these cases, it is convenient to utilize electronic calculators or logarithmic forms of the problem equations.

2. Deferred Annuities. In most of the examples of annuity problems covered in this chapter, the rents occurred over the entire *relevant* period of time. This condition does *not* hold in all business applications. For example, we can modify Example 4 (the PV of annuity) such that the $4,000 expected annual increments to income will begin in the third year of operation of the machine. That is, use of the machine will produce a break-even situation for two years before becoming profitable for the next four years. Therefore, if the machine has a six-year estimated useful life, one should be willing to pay today the present value of the *deferred* stream of $4,000 annual rents. If you require a 10% annual rate of return on investments in assets of this type, you should offer exactly $10,479 for the machine. The solution proceeds as follows:

Step 1—Diagram the problem.

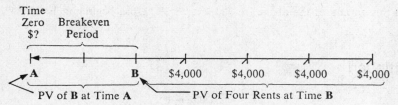

Step 2—Write the *equation* to define the problem.

PV of 4 rents of $4,000 each, deferred two periods = $4,000 × PV of 4 rents of 1 each at 10% (this *discounts* the $4,000 rents back to point **B** above) × PV of 1 at 10% for two periods (this *discounts* the PV of the annuity at **B** back to a PV at point **A**).

Step 3—Identify known and unknown values, insert known values into the equation, and solve for the unknown (present) value. Solutions to deferred annuity problems such as this involve a two-stage process.

$$\text{Maximum to be paid} = \overbrace{\$4,000 \times 3.16987 \text{ (from Table 6-4)}}^{\text{PV of Annuity}} \times \overbrace{.82645 \text{ (from Table 6-2)}}^{\text{PV of 1}}$$
$$= \$10,479$$

Therefore a company that (*a*) estimates the income stream from using a machine as above and (*b*) requires a 10% rate of return on investments in this type of asset should be willing to pay a maximum of $10,479 for this machine.

(Questions for this Frame appear on page 44.)

Answer frame 3⁶

1. False. Assets can be appropriately priced at the PV of cash flows necessary to pay for the asset.
2. True. This distinction also holds for FA of ordinary annuities and FA of annuities due.
3. True. Cost is $4,031, computed as follows:

   Step 1:

   Cost = $?

   +$1,500 $1,000 $1,000 $1,000

   Steps 2 and 3:

   $$\text{Cost} = \$1,500 + (\$1,000 \times 2.53129) \text{ (from Table 6–4)}$$
   $$= \$4,031$$

4. False. Cost is $4,223, computed in the same manner followed in Question 3. The difference is that the interest rate per six-month period is 5%. Therefore, the present value factor from Table 6–4 is 2.72325, the PV of an annuity of three rents of 1 each at 5% *per interest period*. The entire equation is:

   $$\text{Cost} = \$1,500 + (\$1,000 \times 2.72325)$$
   $$= \$4,223$$

If you missed any of the above, reread Frame 3⁶ before beginning Frame 4⁶, page 40.

Frame 4⁶ continued

Table 6–1

Amount of 1, $a = (1 + i)^n$

Periods	5%	6%	7%	8%	9%	10%
1	1.05000	1.06000	1.07000	1.08000	1.09000	1.10000
2	1.10250	1.12360	1.14490	1.16640	1.18810	1.21000
3	1.15762	1.19102	1.22504	1.25971	1.29503	1.33100
4	1.21551	1.26248	1.31080	1.36049	1.41158	1.46410
5	1.27628	1.33823	1.40255	1.46933	1.53862	1.61051
6	1.34010	1.41852	1.50073	1.58687	1.67710	1.77156
7	1.40710	1.50363	1.60578	1.71382	1.82804	1.94872
8	1.47746	1.59385	1.71819	1.85093	1.99256	2.14359
9	1.55133	1.68948	1.83846	1.99900	2.17189	2.35795
10	1.62889	1.79085	1.96715	2.15892	2.36736	2.59374
11	1.71034	1.89830	2.10485	2.33164	2.58043	2.85312
12	1.79586	2.01220	2.25219	2.51817	2.81266	3.13843
13	1.88565	2.13293	2.40985	2.71962	3.06580	3.45227
14	1.97993	2.26090	2.57853	2.93719	3.34173	3.79750
15	2.07893	2.39656	2.75903	3.17217	3.64248	4.17725
16	2.18287	2.54035	2.95216	3.42594	3.97031	4.59497
17	2.29202	2.69277	3.15882	3.70002	4.32763	5.05447
18	2.40662	2.85434	3.37993	3.99602	4.71712	5.55992
19	2.52695	3.02560	3.61653	4.31570	5.14166	6.11591
20	2.65330	3.20714	3.86968	4.66096	5.60441	6.72750
21	2.78596	3.39956	4.14056	5.03383	6.10881	7.40025
22	2.92526	3.60354	4.43040	5.43654	6.65860	8.14027
23	3.07152	3.81975	4.74053	5.87146	7.25787	8.95430
24	3.22510	4.04893	5.07237	6.34118	7.91108	9.84973
25	3.38635	4.29187	5.42743	6.84848	8.62308	10.83471

Table 6–2

Present Value of 1, $p = \dfrac{1}{(1+i)^n}$

Periods	5%	6%	7%	8%	9%	10%
1	.95238	.94340	.93458	.92593	.91743	.90909
2	.90703	.89000	.87344	.85734	.84168	.82645
3	.86384	.83962	.81630	.79383	.77218	.75131
4	.82270	.79209	.76290	.73503	.70843	.68301
5	.78353	.74726	.71299	.68058	.64993	.62092
6	.74622	.70496	.66634	.63017	.59627	.56447
7	.71068	.66506	.62275	.58349	.54703	.51316
8	.67684	.62741	.58201	.54027	.50187	.46651
9	.64461	.59190	.54393	.50025	.46043	.42410
10	.61391	.55839	.50835	.46319	.42241	.38554
11	.58468	.52679	.47509	.42888	.38753	.35049
12	.55684	.49697	.44401	.39711	.35553	.31863
13	.53032	.46884	.41496	.36770	.32618	.28966
14	.50507	.44230	.38782	.34046	.29925	.26333
15	.48102	.41727	.36245	.31524	.27454	.23939
16	.45811	.39365	.33873	.29189	.25187	.21763
17	.43630	.37136	.31657	.27027	.23107	.19784
18	.41552	.35034	.29586	.25025	.21199	.17986
19	.39573	.33051	.27651	.23171	.19449	.16351
20	.37689	.31180	.25842	.21455	.17843	.14864
21	.35894	.29416	.24151	.19866	.16370	.13513
22	.34185	.27751	.22571	.18394	.15018	.12285
23	.32557	.26180	.21095	.17032	.13778	.11168
24	.31007	.24698	.19715	.15770	.12640	.10153
25	.29530	.23300	.18425	.14602	.11597	.09230

Table 6–3

Amount of Annuity of 1, $A_o = \dfrac{(1+i)^n - 1}{i}$

Periodic Rents	5%	6%	7%	8%	9%	10%
1	1.00000	1.00000	1.00000	1.00000	1.00000	1.00000
2	2.05000	2.06000	2.07000	2.08000	2.09000	2.10000
3	3.15250	3.18360	3.21490	3.24640	3.27810	3.31000
4	4.31012	4.37462	4.43994	4.50611	4.57313	4.64100
5	5.52563	5.63709	5.75074	5.86660	5.98471	6.10510
6	6.80191	6.97532	7.15329	7.33593	7.52333	7.71561
7	8.14201	8.39384	8.65402	8.92280	9.20043	9.48717
8	9.54911	9.89747	10.25980	10.63663	11.02847	11.43589
9	11.02656	11.49132	11.97799	12.48756	13.02104	13.57948
10	12.57789	13.18079	13.81645	14.48656	15.19293	15.93742
11	14.20679	14.97164	15.78360	16.64549	17.56029	18.53117
12	15.91713	16.86994	17.88845	18.97713	20.14072	21.38428
13	17.71298	18.88214	20.14064	21.49530	22.95338	24.52271
14	19.59863	21.01507	22.55049	24.21492	26.01919	27.97498
15	21.57856	23.27597	25.12902	27.15211	29.36092	31.77248
16	23.65749	25.67253	27.88805	30.32428	33.00340	35.94973
17	25.84037	28.21288	30.84022	33.75023	36.97370	40.54470
18	28.13238	30.90565	33.99903	37.45024	41.30134	45.59917
19	30.53900	33.75999	37.37896	41.44626	46.01846	51.15909
20	33.06595	36.78559	40.99549	45.76196	51.16012	57.27500
21	35.71925	39.99273	44.86518	50.42292	56.76453	64.00250
22	38.50521	43.39229	49.00574	55.45676	62.87334	71.40275
23	41.43048	46.99583	53.43614	60.89330	69.53194	79.54302
24	44.50200	50.81558	58.17667	66.76476	76.78981	88.49733
25	47.72710	54.86451	63.24904	73.10594	84.70090	98.34706

Table 6–4

Present Value of Annuity of 1, $P_o = \dfrac{1 - \dfrac{1}{(1 + i)^n}}{i}$

Periodic Rents	5%	6%	7%	8%	9%	10%
1	.95238	.94340	.93458	.92593	.91743	.90909
2	1.85941	1.83339	1.80802	1.78326	1.75911	1.73554
3	2.72325	2.67301	2.62432	2.57710	2.53129	2.48685
4	3.54595	3.46511	3.38721	3.31213	3.23972	3.16987
5	4.32948	4.21236	4.10020	3.99271	3.88965	3.79079
6	5.07569	4.91732	4.76654	4.62288	4.48592	4.35526
7	5.78637	5.58238	5.38929	5.20637	5.03295	4.86842
8	6.46321	6.20979	5.97130	5.74664	5.53482	5.33493
9	7.10782	6.80169	6.51523	6.24689	5.99525	5.75902
10	7.72173	7.36009	7.02358	6.71008	6.41766	6.14457
11	8.30641	7.88687	7.49867	7.13896	6.80519	6.49506
12	8.86325	8.38384	7.94269	7.53608	7.16073	6.81369
13	9.39357	8.85268	8.35765	7.90378	7.48690	7.10336
14	9.89864	9.29498	8.74547	8.24424	7.78615	7.36669
15	10.37966	9.71225	9.10791	8.55948	8.06069	7.60608
16	10.83777	10.10590	9.44665	8.85137	8.31256	7.82371
17	11.27407	10.47726	9.76322	9.12164	8.54363	8.02155
18	11.68959	10.82760	10.05909	9.37189	8.75563	8.20141
19	12.08532	11.15812	10.33560	9.60360	8.95011	8.36492
20	12.46221	11.46992	10.59401	9.81815	9.12855	8.51356
21	12.82115	11.76408	10.83553	10.01680	9.29224	8.64869
22	13.16300	12.04158	11.06124	10.20074	9.44243	8.77154
23	13.48857	12.30338	11.27219	10.37106	9.58021	8.88322
24	13.79864	12.55036	11.46933	10.52876	9.70661	8.98474
25	14.09394	12.78336	11.65358	10.67478	9.82258	9.07704

Answer each of the following true-false questions.

_____ 1. If interest is stated at 8% per annum and the interest is compounded monthly, the *effective* interest rate is greater than 8% per annum.

_____ 2. The present value of a deferred annuity will always be greater than the present value of an ordinary annuity—as long as the interest rate is positive.

Work the following problem:

3. Haley Corporation has $20,000 to invest today (beginning of year) in a project that can be expected to break even for the first year. By the end of Year 2, and for each of three years thereafter, the project is expected to earn the target rate of 8%. What will annual income for the Years 2–5 have to be to achieve this goal?

Now check your answers by comparing them to Answer Frame 4[6], page 46.

chapter 7

CASH, SHORT-TERM INVESTMENTS, AND RECEIVABLES

Frame 1[7]

Composition of Cash

The amount of cash reported as a *current asset* on the balance sheet includes the total of coins, currency, bank checking account balances, petty cash funds, and certain types of formal negotiable documents (transferable by endorsement) such as bank drafts, cashier's checks, money orders, certified checks, and ordinary personal checks. Items that should be *excluded* from cash are postage stamps, cash-due memos, IOUs, and checks of customers returned by the bank. Balances in savings accounts, time certificates of deposit, and similar items should not be reported as cash but as investments. Sound internal control requires that (*a*) all cash receipts be deposited in the bank and (*b*) all cash disbursements be made by check.

Petty Cash

In companies where all payments are made by check, frequently there is a need for a small fund of cash to be kept on hand to make miscellaneous small payments for postage, newspapers, and so forth. To meet this need, a *petty cash* system, including suitable controls, should be established. To illustrate the procedure, assume the following events:

a. Establishment of a $100 petty cash fund. The entry is:

Petty cash	100	
Cash		100

b. Disbursement of $38.16 from petty cash fund for postage of $10 and supplies of $28.16.

No entry.

c. Replenishment of the fund—to the established balance of $100, at the end of the period. The entry is:

Miscellaneous expense	10.00	
Office supplies	28.16	
Cash		38.16

The replenishment entry must be made before financial statements are prepared in order to bring the petty cash *fund* into agreement with the Petty Cash account, which was established at $100.

Answer frame 4⁶

1. True. The effective interest rate is 8.30% $\left[\left(1 + \frac{.08}{12}\right)^{12} - 1\right]$.

2. False. The present value of a deferred annuity will always be *less* than the present value of an ordinary annuity—with a positive interest rate—because of the (additional) discounting of the present value of the annuity.

3. $6,521. This is a PV of a deferred annuity problem. The solution proceeds as follows:

    Diagram:

    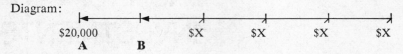

    | $20,000 | | $X | $X | $X | $X |
    | A | B | | | | |

    Equations:

    First, solve for the value of the investment at point **B.** This determination involves the FA of $20,000 at 8% for one period. Therefore, the value at **B** is $21,600 ($20,000 × 1.08).

    Second, solve for the (unknown) annual rents ($X above) using:

    a. $21,600, the present value of the annuity, and
    b.   3.31213 (from Table 6–4), the present value of four rents of one each at 8%.

    This second equation is:

    $$\$21,600 = \$X \times 3.31213$$
    $$\$X = \$21,600 \div 3.31213$$
    $$= \$6,521$$

    This problem illustrates a very important point that is germane to *all* present value and future amount problems. It should be obvious (if not *altogether* clear) that, as long as one interest rate pertains to all periods in a problem situation, it is possible to measure present value or future amount at any point on the continuum as an intermediate step toward solving a particular problem. As long as the same interest rate pertains to all periods, the present value given in a problem can be carried forward to a future amount or the future amount can be discounted back to a present value at any point on the continuum. And the computed value or amount at the intermediate date is identically equal to the present value at the left extreme of the continuum *and* to the future amount at the right extreme of the continuum. This is the nature of present value and future amount.

If you missed any of the above questions, you should reread Frame 4⁶ before proceeding.

You have now completed Chapter 6. Chapters 1–6 have contained a review of the accounting model, the end-of-the-period adjusting and closing processes, the primary financial statements, and present value concepts. You should now take Sample Examination 1 that covers Chapters 1–6, beginning on page 125.

Then continue reading with Chapter 7. Chapters 7–11 cover the "current" accounts —assets (Chapters 7–10) and liabilities (Chapter 11). Then Chapters 12–14 cover long-term operational assets. Chapters 15–25 (Volume II) cover the equity (i.e., right-hand) side of the balance sheet—liabilities and stockholders' equity—plus a variety of more general topics.

Frame 1[7] continued
Bank Reconciliations

Once each month a *bank statement* is received. The bank statement includes all deposit slips and all checks paid by the bank and posted to the depositor's account during the month. The bank statement shows the beginning bank balance, the deposits recorded, the checks paid, other debit and credit memoranda, and the ending bank balance for the month. The ending balance reported by the bank statement seldom agrees with the ending balance reflected by the company in its Cash account. Therefore a *bank reconciliation* must be developed to bring the two ending balances into agreement as far as the records are concerned; some of the reasons for the differences between the two balances will require entries in the accounts by the company. To illustrate, assume the following relevant data from the *two* sources indicated were on hand at the end of a particular month:

From the Bank Statement		*From the Accounting Records*	
Ending balance in bank	$1,394	Ending balance in regular cash account	$1,435
Bank service charges for the month .	14	Cash on hand (petty cash) . . .	100
Interest income on note collected by the bank for our account	20	Unrecorded deposits—deposits sent to bank on last day of month, after bank statement was prepared . .	450
		Outstanding checks—checks written and released (mailed) but not paid by the bank before bank statement was prepared	403

With these data, a bank reconciliation can be prepared; the following form is recommended:

Bank			*Books*	
Ending bank balance . .		$1,394	Ending book balance ($1,435 + $100)	$1,535
Additions:			Additions:	
Unrecorded deposit . . .	$450		Interest collected by bank . . .	20
Cash on hand	100	550		1,555
		1,944	Deductions:	
Deductions:			Bank charges	14
Outstanding checks . . .		403		
Correct cash balance (for balance sheet)		$1,541 ◄————————————►	Correct cash balance	$1,541

Note that in the above reconciliation we were careful to enter the differences under the respective captions so that the final amount for *both* "Bank" and "Books" represents the amount of *cash* that should be reported on the balance sheet; that is, we entered:

a. Under "Bank" only those items that would be reflected in the bank balance, assuming *all* deposits (including petty cash) and all checks written were *included* on the bank statement.
b. Under "Books" *all* items that would be entered in the Cash account if it were completely up to date.

For balance sheet purposes we want the cash amount reported to be *up to date;* therefore, we must make an entry in the accounts for *each* of the changes listed under "Books." The entries would be:

Cash	20	
Interest revenue		20

Miscellaneous expense (for bank service charge)	14	
Cash		14

Having made these entries in the accounting records, the Cash account (plus the *Petty Cash* account) will show the correct cash balance of $1,541 and this amount will be reported on the balance sheet.

Is each of the following statements true or false?

_____ 1. A firm that includes "hot" checks from customers in its Cash account balance overstates the Cash balance reported on the balance sheet.

_____ 2. Company A set up a $500 petty cash account. This means that the Petty Cash account reported on the balance sheet will always have a $500 balance.

_____ 3. Companies may use the *bank* side of their bank reconciliation as a source for certain book entries.

_____ 4. A company has the following data available for purposes of preparing its bank reconciliation as of January 19, 19A:

Balance per books on January 19, 19A	$1,500
Balance per bank statement on January 19, 19A	1,365
Deposits in transit (i.e., not recorded by bank) at January 19, 19A . . .	220
Bank service charge included on January 19, 19A bank statement . . .	6

If these are the only reconciling items besides outstanding checks, and if the corrected cash balance is $1,494, outstanding checks must be $85.

Now compare your responses with those given in Answer Frame 1[7], page 50.

Frame 2[7]

Short-Term Investments

There are three types of investments in the accounting context: (*a*) short-term investments, (*b*) long-term investments, and (*c*) controlling interests in other corporations (over 50% of the voting stock owned). The last two categories are considered in Chapter 18.

A company frequently has idle cash, and to realize some return on it the management may purchase marketable securities; such short-term *investments* are reported on the balance sheet as current assets. An investment, to be short-term, must meet *both* of the following criteria:

a. Marketability—there must be a ready market for the securities.
b. Management intention—it must be the intention of the management of the company to convert the securities back to cash during the upcoming operating cycle.

Short-Term Investments in Stock

Short-term investments in stock are recorded initially at *cost* in conformance with the cost principle; subsequent to acquisition they are required by FASB *Statement No. 12* to be carried at the *lower* of cost or market. Cost includes the purchase price plus brokerage costs, taxes, and all other costs incidental to acquisition. To illustrate the treatment of short-term investments in stock, assume that Company A purchased the following stocks as short-term investments:

a. 100 shares of X Corporation stock at $76.
b. 200 shares of Y Corporation stock at $40 plus incidental costs of $100.

The entry to record the acquisition would be:

Short-term investments in stocks [($76 × 100) + ($40 × 200) + $100]	15,700	
Cash		15,700

The entry to record receipt of a dividend of $3 per share on the X Corporation stock would be:

Cash 300
    Investment revenue 300

Valuation of short-term investments at the lower of cost or market is justified on the basis that when there has been a significant decline in the value of a *current asset* it should be recognized. In applying the lower-of-cost-or-market rule, the entire *portfolio* of short-term investments in stocks is considered as a unit (as opposed to item-by-item consideration, as is often done with inventory).

Assume at the end of the first accounting period X Corporation shares are selling at $77 and Y Corporation shares are selling at $30; the entry to record the lower of cost or market (LCM) would be:

Unrealized loss due to reduction of short-term investments from cost to
    market value 2,000
    Allowance to reduce short-term investments to LCM 2,000
Computations:

	Cost	Market	Difference
X Corporation stock (100 shares) . . .	$ 7,600	$ 7,700	
Y Corporation stock (200 shares) . . .	8,100	6,000	
Totals	$15,700	$13,700	$2,000

At this point the balance sheet would report the marketable securities as follows:

Current Assets:
Short-term investments at lower of cost or market (cost $15,700) $13,700

The income statement for the first accounting period would report the Unrealized Loss account, which like other income statement accounts is closed into the Income Summary at the end of the period.

Now assume further that 100 shares of Y Corporation stock are subsequently sold at $35; the entry to record the sale would be:

Cash (100 × $35) 3,500
Loss on sale of short-term investments 550
    Short-term investments in stocks ($8,100 × ½) 4,050

Note that the gain or loss on disposition of short-term investments is measured as the difference between proceeds and *cost*. Therefore, the allowance account is not adjusted at the time of the disposition of shares from the short-term portfolio. Rather, the $2,000 credit balance in the Allowance to Reduce Short-Term Investments to LCM will be "corrected" by the next end-of-the-period adjusting entry.

Short-Term Investments in Bonds

The above illustration included only *stocks* in the portfolio; when *bonds* are purchased, the additional problem of interest revenue must be considered. Dividends on stocks are never *accrued* (there is no obligation to pay dividends until they are declared), whereas interest on bonds must be accrued (since it legally accrues with the passage of time). But accrued interest on a bond investment is not part of the *cost* of the investments. Furthermore, FASB *Statement No. 12* does not apply to short-term bond investments. Nevertheless, short-term investments in bonds should be accounted for at the lower of cost or market—where the lower market value is other than day-to-day price movements. This method of accounting for short-term bond investments accords with the provisions of *Accounting Research Bulletin No. 43*.

To illustrate the purchase of bonds as a short-term investment, assume the purchase on May 1 of six bonds of Z Corporation at 102, each having a maturity value of $1,000 and an 8% annual interest rate payable semiannually on April 1 and October 1. The accounting period ends on December 31. The indicated entries would be:

Answer frame 1⁷

1. True. These "hot" checks are properly classified as accounts receivable because the customer's bank has not given us cash yet. Therefore, inclusion of "hot" checks from customers in Cash overstates Cash and understates Accounts Receivable.
2. True. Unless the established balance is changed.
3. False. The bank side includes items that have already been recorded on the books but not yet recorded on the bank statement. By contrast, reconciling items such as bank collections on our behalf, bank service charges, and customer "hot" checks will appear on the book side of the bank reconciliation because the bank has already included them on the bank statement. Therefore, companies make book entries for items on the *book* side of the bank reconciliation.
4. False. The outstanding checks must be $91, computed as follows:

Bank		*Books*	
Balance 1/1/19A	$1,365	Balance 1/1/19A	$1,500
Add deposits in transit	+ 220	Deduct bank service charge	− 6
Deduct outstanding checks	− X		
Corrected bank balance	$1,494	Corrected book balance	$1,494

$$\$1,365 + \$220 - X = \$1,494$$
$$- X = \$1,494 - \$1,365 - \$220$$
$$X = \$91$$

Therefore, outstanding checks must be $91.
If you missed any of the above, reread Frame 1⁷ before beginning Frame 2⁷, page 48.

Frame 2⁷ continued

a. May 1—To record the purchase of six bonds at 102; one month's accrued interest:

Short-term investments in bonds	6,120	
Interest revenue ($6,000 × 8% × $\frac{1}{12}$)	40	
Cash		6,160

b. October 1—To record collection of six months' interest:

Cash ($6,000 × 8% × $\frac{6}{12}$)	240	
Interest revenue		240

c. December 31—To accrue three months' interest income:

Interest receivable ($6,000 × 8% × $\frac{3}{12}$)	120	
Interest revenue		120

December 31—To close Interest Revenue:

Interest revenue ($240 + $120 − $40)	320	
Income summary*		320

     * Verification: The bonds have been held 8 months (May 1–December 31); therefore, interest revenue is ($6,000 × 8% × $\frac{8}{12}$) = $320.

Note that premium (or discount) on the purchase of a bond as a short-term investment is not amortized as would be done if it were a *long-term investment*. This procedure is acceptable since there are no plans to keep the bond to maturity. For a review of long-term investments in bonds, see Chapter 19.

True or false?

_____ 1. The unit of analysis for purposes of applying the lower-of-cost-or-market valuation to short-term investments in stocks is the individual issue held.

_____ 2. Company G purchased 1,000-share investments in each of two stocks: A and B. The A stock cost $75 per share, and the B stock cost $12 per share. At year-end, the two stocks were quoted in the *Wall Street Journal* at $73 for A and $15 for B. Accordingly, Company G should report short-term investments at $88,000.

_____ 3. When a bond investment is purchased "plus accrued interest," this implies a need to debit Interest Revenue to record the acquisition of the investment.

_____ 4. When a bond investment is purchased "plus accrued interest," this implies that the *cost* of the investment includes the interest.

Now check your answers with those given in Answer Frame 2[7], page 52.

Frame 3[7]

Nature of Receivables

Broadly speaking, receivables represent claims of the entity against others for money, goods, or services. For accounting and reporting purposes receivables must be classified according to type; thus, the principal categories of receivables are (*a*) trade receivables (from regular customers), comprised of accounts receivable and notes receivable; and (*b*) special receivables comprised of claims against debtors other than trade customers; for example, advances to employees, and deposits made with others (such as a utility deposit). Receivables, on an item-by-item basis, must be classified as either current assets or noncurrent assets, depending on their characteristics, and they are reported on the balance sheet.

Accounts Receivable (trade)

"Accounts receivable" is the term commonly used to designate that class of receivables due from regular customers and arising from the sale of goods or services on credit. Such receivables are accounted for and reported at their expected realizable value, since they are current assets. This is accomplished by utilizing an account such as Allowance for Doubtful Accounts (or Allowance for Bad Debts), which is a contra (credit balance) asset account that is reported as a deduction from the asset account, Accounts Receivable. Since practically all firms that extend credit will suffer some credit losses through uncollectible accounts (bad debts), an accounting procedure has been developed for this situation. It is important to note that the "bad debt" procedure has two effects, viz:

a. It *matches* estimated bad debt expense with current sales revenue. The credit sales for any particular period give rise to some credit losses, the exact amount of which will be determined in future periods when the account cannot be collected. However, these losses should be *matched* with the sales revenue that gave rise to them. In order to accomplish this, the amount of bad debt loss must be estimated each period.

b. It serves to "carry" accounts receivable at the estimated net realizable value.

To illustrate, assume Baker Company sold $100,000 worth of goods on credit during 19A and that on the basis of past experience 1% of all credit sales are never collected. At the end of 19A the following *adjusting* entry for *estimated* bad debts would be made:

Answer frame 2[7]

1. False. The unit of analysis for this purpose is the entire portfolio of stocks held as *short-term* investments.
2. False. Company G should report short-term investments at cost of $87,000 because market of $88,000 is greater than cost.
3. True. This debit to Interest Revenue will be offset by the credit to Interest Revenue that is recorded upon receipt of interest on the next full-period interest date.
4. False. The cash outlay includes (*a*) the cost of the bond investment plus (*b*) the accrued interest. But *cost* does *not* include the accrued interest.

If you missed any of the above, reread Frame 2[7] before beginning Frame 3[7], page 51.

Frame 3[7] continued

Bad debt expense (estimated)	1,000	
Allowance for doubtful accounts (bad debts)		1,000

Now assume it is three years later (19D) and that A. B. Racy, who purchased $150 worth of goods on credit in 19A, refused to pay his account; collection efforts have been unsuccessful, and the management decides to write off his account as a loss. The following entry would be made:

Allowance for doubtful accounts	150	
Accounts receivable (A. B. Racy)		150

You should note that the first entry (in 19A) had two effects: (*a*) it reduced reported income for 19A by $1,000 and (*b*) it reduced the net amount of accounts receivable reported on the balance sheet by $1,000. You also should note that the second entry (in 19D) had the following effects: (*a*) no effect on the income statement for 19D; (*b*) no effect on the net accounts receivable on the 19D balance sheet; and (*c*) its only effect was to reduce the debit balance in Accounts Receivable and the credit balance in the Allowance account by $150. Since the allowance account is subtracted from Accounts Receivable, the entry did not change the *difference* between them; thus, the impact of credit losses was recorded and reported only in 19A.

Methods of Estimating Bad Debts

The above entries illustrate one method of *estimating* the dollar amount of Bad Debt Expense and the related balance in the Allowance for Doubtful Accounts. The method illustrated involves estimation of *Bad Debt Expense* as a percent of *credit sales*. Thus, the focus is on the expenses account, although the allowance account is also affected by the expense entry (see above). To apply the percent-of-sales method, the estimated bad debt percentage should be multiplied by *credit* sales (rather than *cash* or *total* sales) because only *credit* sales cause bad debt losses.

The other principal method of arriving at the dollar estimate focuses on the allowance account. That is, rather than *directly* estimating *bad debt expense,* it estimates the balance needed in the *allowance* account to properly value net accounts receivable. This method is operationalized by "aging" individual customers' accounts receivable accounts and applying predicted loss rate percentages to the various "ages" of individual accounts. Illustration 7–1 presents an aging of total accounts receivable of $40,000 as of December 31, 19A. Illustration 7–2 reveals that $3,250 is estimated to be the credit balance needed in the allowance account to reduce net accounts receivable, as reported on the balance sheet, to net realizable value of $36,750 ($40,000 − $3,250).

Therefore, if we assume that prior to aging accounts receivable the Allowance for Doubtful Accounts already had a credit balance of $1,500, the following entry would be required:

Bad debt expense	1,750	
Allowance for doubtful accounts ($3,250 − $1,500)		1,750

Illustration 7-1

Aged Accounts Receivable at 12/31/19A

Customer	Receivable Balance 12/31/19A	Not Past Due	Past Due		
			1–30 Days	31–60 Days	Over 60 Days
Able	$ 3,000		$2,000	$ 850	$150
Baker	7,000	$ 7,000			
Cox	4,500	3,000	1,000	450	50
Young	1,000	500	200		$100
Totals	$40,000	$32,000	$5,000	$2,500	$500

Illustration 7-2

Determination of Estimated Bad Debt Loss on Accounts Receivable

Status	Balances from Aging Schedule	Experience Loss Percentages	Balance Required in Allowance Account
Not past due	$32,000	5%	$1,600
1–30 days past due	5,000	10	500
31–60 days past due	2,500	30	750
Over 60 days past due . . .	500	80	400
	$40,000		$3,250

The reader should observe that this entry debits and credits the same accounts as those debited and credited in the bad debt entry given at top of page 52. The only difference involves the method of estimating the dollar amount of the entry. Furthermore, the entry to write off individual customers' accounts which are bad is also the same as the one given on page 52.

Determine whether each of the following statements is true or false.

_____ 1. Accounts receivable should be reported on the balance sheet at face (i.e., maturity) value.

_____ 2. Bad Debt Expense is not an operating expense account because it must be estimated.

_____ 3. If at the end of a period (a) the Allowance for Doubtful Accounts has a credit balance of $1,000, (b) the percent-of-credit-sales method is used to estimate credit losses at 2%, and (c) credit sales total $200,000 for the period, the ending balance in the Allowance account will be $5,000.

_____ 4. Now modify the facts given in Question 3 above to include a year-end write-off of $1,500 of uncollectible accounts. Total accounts receivable prior to the write-off are $95,000. After the $1,500 write-off, net accounts receivable will be $88,500.

Now compare your answers with those given in Answer Frame 3[7], page 54.

Answer frame 3⁷

1. False. Accounts receivable should be reported at *net* realizable value, that is, Accounts Receivable account balance less the credit balance in Allowance for Doubtful Accounts.
2. False. It *is* an operating expense. Depreciation expense and warranty expense are other operating expenses that must also be estimated.
3. True. The current period addition to the Allowance account is $4,000 (2% × $200,000). This $4,000 plus the preexisting balance of $1,000 produces an ending balance of $5,000 in the Allowance account.
4. False. *Net* Accounts Receivable will be $90,000, as evidenced from the T-accounts below:

Accounts Receivable		Allowance for Doubtful Accounts	
95,000	1,500	Write off of uncollectibles 1,500	1,000 balance before year-end addition
93,500			4,000 (2% × $200,000) year-end addition
			3,500

Net Accounts Receivable = $90,000 ($93,500 − $3,500)

If you missed any of the above, reread Frame 3⁷ before beginning Frame 4⁷, below.

Frame 4⁷

Special Receivables

All receivables, other than *trade* accounts receivable, are generally classified as special; they should be classified as current assets only if they accord with the definition of current assets previously given. Special receivables should be reported in the financial statements separately from accounts receivable.

Notes Receivable

Notes receivable may consist of trade notes receivable (from regular customers) and special notes receivable (from other sources). Short-term notes receivable should be classified as current assets, long-term notes receivable as *other assets*. Practically all notes involve interest, although those wherein the interest is taken out in advance frequently are labeled as noninterest bearing. Interest usually is calculated on the basis of a 360-day year. Thus, interest on a $2,000, 7½%, 120-day interest-bearing note would be calculated as follows:

$$\$2,000 \times .075 \times \frac{120}{360} = \$50$$

Assuming this note was received in settlement of a $2,000 account receivable, the entry would be:

Notes receivable (trade)	2,000	
Accounts receivable (trade)		2,000

At maturity, receipt of payment would be recorded as follows:

Cash	2,050	
Notes receivable (trade)		2,000
Interest revenue		50

Frequently, a business in need of immediate cash will *discount* one or more of the notes receivable that it holds; this transaction means that the business, in effect, sells the note receivable by endorsing it over to the bank. The maker of the note receivable then pays the bank at maturity. The endorser of the note (a negotiable instrument) is legally liable for payment should the maker default; that is, the endorser has a *contingent liability* from the date of endorsement until the maturity date of the note. To illustrate the discounting of a note receivable, assume that the above note, after being held for 30 days, was discounted at the bank at 9% interest. Entries and computations to follow this note through several potential events are given below.

a. To record the discounting transaction:
   Computations:

$$\text{Maturity value} \left(\$2,000 \times .075 \times \frac{120}{360} \right) = \$50 + \$2,000 \quad . \quad . \quad . \quad . \quad . \quad \$2,050.00$$

$$\text{Discount (interest charged by bank)} - \$2,050 \times .09 \times \frac{90}{360} . \quad . \quad . \quad . \quad 46.13$$

Difference—Cash Proceeds from Bank $2,003.87

   Entry:

Cash	2,003.87	
Notes receivable discounted (or notes receivable)		2,000.00
Interest revenue		3.87

Assuming a balance sheet was prepared at this point in time, the discounted note would be reported as follows:

Current Assets:
   Notes receivable $2,000
      Less: Notes receivable discounted . . 2,000 $ –0–

b. Assuming the maker paid the bank in full ($2,050) on the due date, the endorser would make the following entry:

Notes receivable discounted	2,000	
Notes receivable		2,000

c. Instead, now assume that the maker defaulted and the endorser had to pay the bank for the note. In this case the following entry would be made:

Note receivable discounted (name)	2,000	
Accounts receivable (or dishonored notes receivable)	2,050	
Note receivable		2,000
Cash		2,050

Note that at this point in time the records would not show a note receivable but rather would show an account receivable for the note plus the interest ($2,050). The dishonored note would be held as evidence of the debt.

Sale and Pledging of Accounts Receivable

Companies frequently utilize accounts receivable to secure immediate cash prior to the regular collection date. The discussion that follows is therefore conceptually very similar to discounting notes receivable in order to obtain immediate cash. There are four separate types of transactions that achieve this end; they are reviewed below.

Pledging Accounts Receivable. Loans are sometimes obtained from banks and other lenders by pledging accounts receivable as security. The borrower who has pledged his receivables continues to collect the receivables but is required to apply the collections on the loan until it is repaid. When accounts receivable are pledged, no entry is made in the accounts; however, full disclosure requires appropriate information (footnote) to be disclosed on the balance sheet.

Outright Sale of Accounts Receivable. Occasionally accounts receivable are literally sold to a third party (usually at a substantial discount) without recourse. The purchaser of the receivables assumes all collection costs and risks. Sale of accounts receivable usually occurs only when a business is in serious financial difficulties. To illustrate, assume L Company sold $10,000 of its accounts receivable (with an associated allowance for doubtful accounts of $500) at 60 percent of their recorded value. The entry would be:

Cash	6,000	
Allowance for doubtful accounts	500	
Financing expenses	3,500	
Accounts receivable		10,000

Assignment of Accounts Receivable.   In this situation accounts receivable are sold on a "with recourse, nonnotification" basis; that is, the borrower retains all risks of bad debt losses on the receivables assigned, and the customer who owes the receivables never knows of the assignment. To illustrate the assignment procedure, the following entries and explanations are presented:

1.   Brown Retailers are short of cash; as a consequence they have assigned $40,000 accounts receivable on a "with recourse, nonnotification" (assignment) basis to the Super Finance Corporation. They received, per the contract, 85% of the recorded value of the receivables, or $34,000, and signed a note payable for this amount. Super will bill the finance charges each month. Entries to record the assignment:

a.   To set up the assigned accounts in a separate account:

Accounts receivable assigned	40,000	
Accounts receivable		40,000

b.   To record receipt of cash and to set up a liability account (which is a contra account to Accounts Receivable Assigned):

Cash ($40,000 × 85%)	34,000	
Note payable		34,000

2.   A summary of transactions during the first month showed the following:

Cash on assigned accounts collected and remitted to Super	$29,700
Sales returns on assigned accounts	500
Sales discounts on assigned accounts	300
Total	$30,500
Finance charges billed by Super Finance	$250

a.   The entry to record collections on assigned accounts receivable:

Cash	29,700	
Sales returns	500	
Sales discounts	300	
Accounts receivable assigned		30,500

b.   To record remittance to Super Finance:

Note payable	29,700	
Interest expense	250	
Cash		29,950

A balance sheet prepared at this point would show the following:

Accounts receivable assigned ($40,000 − $30,500)	$9,500	
Less: Note payable ($34,000 − $29,700)	4,300	
Equity in assigned accounts receivable		$5,200

Factoring Accounts Receivable. Factoring is very similar to assignment, the primary differences being that (*a*) the lending agency (the factor) advances cash at time of sale; (*b*) the factor passes on the granting of credit to the customer; (*c*) the receivable is sold *without* recourse; and (*d*) the factor collects directly from the customer. This is a very common means of converting a sale on credit into immediate cash.

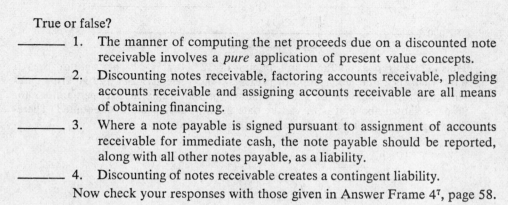

True or false?

———— 1. The manner of computing the net proceeds due on a discounted note receivable involves a *pure* application of present value concepts.

———— 2. Discounting notes receivable, factoring accounts receivable, pledging accounts receivable and assigning accounts receivable are all means of obtaining financing.

———— 3. Where a note payable is signed pursuant to assignment of accounts receivable for immediate cash, the note payable should be reported, along with all other notes payable, as a liability.

———— 4. Discounting of notes receivable creates a contingent liability.

Now check your responses with those given in Answer Frame 4[7], page 58.

Answer frame 4[7]

1. False. To understand this, return to the text example given on page 55. Note in particular that the bank's discount of $46.13 was computed on the entire proceeds of $2,050 (which includes interest of $50 on the note receivable). To see this answer more clearly, consider the pure application of present value diagrammed below:

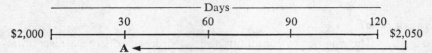

Thus, $2,050 represents the future amount of $2,000 at 7½ % per annum for 120 days. (This is a pure application of present value concepts.) But $2,050 also represents the future amount of some unknown present value at 9% per annum for 90 days, shown above at point **A,** the date the note receivable is discounted. Therefore, applying *pure* present value concepts suggests that:

$$PV \text{ at } \mathbf{A} = \$2,050 \times \frac{1}{\left(1 + \dfrac{.09}{12}\right)^3} \text{ (Equation 2 in Chapter 6)}$$

$$= \$2,050 \times \frac{1}{(1.0075)^3}$$

$$= \$2,050 \times .977833$$

$$= \$2,004.56$$

If the bank had applied pure present value concepts, they would have paid $2,004.56 for the note receivable at point **A** above. Instead they were only willing to pay the $2,003.87 computed on page 55. The difference is very small indeed, but this problem does provide an interesting context for better understanding present value applications to common business problems.

2. True. These are all means of borrowing money.
3. False. The note payable created pursuant to assigning accounts receivable should be reported contra to the assigned accounts receivable because the note payable represents a reduction in the *assignor's* equity in his own accounts receivable. To report this note payable as a liability would inflate both reported assets and reported liabilities.
4. True. The contingent liability exists until the maturity date on the (discounted) note receivable.

If you have missed any of the above questions, you should reread Frame 4[7] before proceeding. Then continue reading with Chapter 8.

chapter 8

INVENTORIES—GENERAL PROBLEMS

Frame 1[8]

Nature of Inventories

One basic purpose in accounting for inventories is the determination of net income through the matching of inventory cost (cost of goods sold) with revenue. As an accounting category, inventory is a current asset represented by goods *owned* by the firm and held for sale or for utilization in the manufacture of goods for sale. Inventories of a manufacturing company are classified as follows:

1. Finished goods inventory—goods held for sale.
2. Raw materials inventory—goods held for direct use in the manufacture of other goods.
3. Goods (work) in process inventory—goods held that are partly processed and which require further processing before sale.
4. Supplies inventory—items held for indirect use in the company such as lubricating oils and office supplies.

A trading company (i.e., not a manufacturer) will have only finished goods inventory and also perhaps an inventory of supplies. There are two basic problems in accounting for inventories:

1. Determination of the physical goods (items and quantities) that should be included in the inventory.
2. Determination of the accounting (dollar) values to be assigned to the goods in inventory.

Determination of Inventory Items and Quantities. All goods which the firm owns (has legal title to) should be included in inventory. The party who pays the freight is assumed to have title during transit; therefore, during transit, goods shipped *f.o.b. destination* are owned by the seller and goods shipped *f.o.b. shipping point* are owned by the buyer. As a practical matter, however, most companies record purchases of inventory when the goods are received—even when the terms are f.o.b. shipping point—because of the increased cost of maintaining records that indicate *when* the supplier shipped the goods. This departure from "perfect" accounting is justified on the basis of materiality.

There are two basic types of inventory accounting systems: *periodic* and *perpetual*. The names of the two systems are indicative of the frequency with which inventory quantities are determined.

Under the *periodic* system, beginning inventory, as reflected in the inventory account in the general ledger, is transferred to income summary at the end of each period as part of the adjusting and closing processes (see Chapter 3) and is not changed during the ensuing period. As a result, *during* any one period, the Inventory account reflects the *beginning* inventory of the period, and no perpetual record of inventories on hand is kept. Then, at the end of the period, a physical count of inventories is made—to arrive at *ending* inventory. This number is then used as the amount for an adjusting entry to record the then-correct ending inventory amount.

Under the *perpetual* system, a running record of inventory on hand (in units and/or dollars) is kept perpetually. The perpetual system involves the use of special subsidiary inventory records that list for each item the quantities acquired, issued, and the quantity on hand. In general, perpetual systems are used for high-unit-value items of inventory, and periodic systems are used for low-unit-value and fungible items of inventory.

Most companies, regardless of the system they employ, usually take a physical count of the inventory at least once a year to check on the accuracy of the inventory records.

The following entries illustrate the accounting for inventories under both systems:

To record purchase of 1,000 units of inventory at a cost (net of purchase discount) of $2 per unit:

Periodic Inventory System		*Perpetual Inventory System*	
Purchases (an expense account) 2,000		Inventory 2,000	
Cash (or accounts payable)	2,000	Cash (or accounts payable)	2,000

To record sale of 800 units at $3 per unit [assume that beginning inventory consisted of 200 units at net unit cost of $1.50 and that the company employs the first-in, first-out flow method (to be covered in Chapter 9)]:

Cash (or accounts receivable) 2,400		Cash (or accounts receivable) 2,400	
Sales revenue (800 × $3) . .	2,400	Sales revenue (800 × $3) . . .	2,400
(No entry.)		Cost of goods sold (200 × $1.50) + (600 × $2) . . 1,500	
		Inventory	1,500

To adjust end-of-period inventory. Assume the physical count reveals 400 units on hand at a unit cost of $2:

Cost of goods sold* ($300 + $2,000 − $800)** . . . 1,500			
Inventory (ending) (400 × $2) 800		(No adjustment needed because Cost of Goods Sold and Ending Inventory have been recorded above under the Perpetual Inventory system.)	
Purchases (from entry above)	2,000		
Inventory (beginning) (200 × $1.50) . .	300		

* Or Income Summary.
** Beginning inventory ($300) + Purchases ($2,000) − Ending inventory ($800).

Note in the above entries that the dollar amounts of ending inventory ($800) and cost of goods sold ($1,500) are the same under both systems. [Ending inventory under the perpetual system is also $800 ($300 + $2,000 − $1,500).]

Determination of Accounting (Dollar) Values. A basic accounting principle is that inventories should be valued at *cost;* however, some exceptions are permitted. Determination of the accounting value of inventory involves two distinct problems, viz:

1. Inventory valuation—selection of an appropriate *unit cost* for each item in the inventory. The principal *inventory valuation methods* are:
    a. Cost basis:
        (1) Historical cost—purchase cost (or cost of manufacturing) plus all incidental costs such as freight-in and *less* purchase discount.

b. Departure from cost basis:

(2) Lower of cost or market—discussed below.

(3) Selling price—permitted only for some commodities for which there is an effective government-controlled market and immediate marketability. Selling price, when used, should be reduced for costs of disposal.

(4) Net realizable value—goods that are damaged, obsolete, or depreciated should be valued at cash sales value less all costs to repair and sell. To illustrate:

Cash sales price of damaged refrigerator		$150
Less: Repair Costs	$30	
Selling costs	20	
Delivery costs	5	55
Net Realizable Value		$ 95

(5) Direct cost—goods manufactured by the firm, valued at *variable* manufacturing costs only (excluding fixed costs), that is, direct material, direct labor, and *variable* factory overhead. To date the "direct costing" method has *not* been accorded general acceptance by the accounting profession. However, it is widely used for *internal* control purposes.

2. Inventory flow—selection of an appropriate *assumed flow* of unit costs during the accounting period; the principal *inventory flow methods* are (discussed in Chapter 9):

a. Specific cost.

b. Average cost.

c. First-in, first-out (Fifo).

d. Last-in, first-out (Lifo).

Effect of Inventory Errors

Inventory is similar to *accruals* and *short-term* deferrals in respect to the effect that inventory accounting errors have on reported income. To see this, consider an accounting error affecting a *long-term* deferral such as Depreciation Expense. Suppose that depreciation expense is erroneously understated in 19B. The 19B income will be overstated, but there will ordinarily be no direct effect on 19C income as a result of the 19B depreciation error.

Next consider an understatement of $1,000 in the 19B ending inventory. This error causes 19B cost of goods sold to be overstated by $1,000, which in turn causes 19B income to be understated by the same amount (ignoring income taxes). The ending 19B inventory then becomes the beginning 19C inventory for purposes of computing 19C cost of goods sold. Therefore, 19C's beginning inventory is understated, which causes 19C cost of goods sold to be understated and this causes 19C income to be overstated by $1,000. From this brief description it is clear that each error involving the ending inventory:

a. Affects income for the year when the error is made *and* also for the next year as well.

b. Is self-correcting when both years (each of which is in error) are considered in the aggregate.

Thus, in the final analysis—that is, after the second year—*total* net income for the two years (and the balance in Retained Earnings at the end of the second year) is correctly stated. This series of effects is similar to that which occurs when an expense is not accrued in a period during which it occurs but rather is recorded in the next accounting period when cash is paid. The same also applies to errors affecting *short-term* prepaid (or deferred) items.

True or false?

_____ 1. Inventories are classified as current assets or operational (fixed) assets depending on the nature of the inventory.

_____ 2. Application of the perpetual inventory system produces more net income than application of the periodic system.

_____ 3. Under the periodic system, the general ledger Inventory account reflects *beginning* inventory even after the beginning of the fiscal year, and then at year-end, the beginning inventory balance is replaced in the account with the ending inventory balance.

_____ 4. If purchases total $20,000, ending inventory $6,000 and cost of goods sold $30,000, then the beginning inventory was $16,000.

_____ 5. If the purchases amount is overstated, this error overstates cost of goods sold for the year the error is made. If the ending inventory for this same year is correctly stated, the error in purchases has no effect on the net income of the next year.

Now compare your answers with those given in Answer Frame 1[8], page 64.

Frame 2[8]

Lower of Cost or Market

It was stated above that inventory is generally valued at cost. In some cases, however, cost may not be an appropriate valuation for inventory. For example, when the current replacement or reproduction cost of items held in inventory is *less* than the original cost of those items, the former should be used for valuation of the inventory. This position has been accepted by the accounting profession on the basis of (*a*) the matching principle, that is, the present economic utility of the goods is less than original cost, hence there has been a *holding loss* which should be recognized in the period in which the decline took place, and the lower current replacement cost of the goods should be matched against revenue realized from their sale; and (*b*) balance sheet conservatism. *Market* in this context is defined as the current bid (i.e., purchase) price prevailing at the date of the inventory for the particular merchandise in the volume in which usually purchased. In applying the lower of cost or market rule three approaches have been suggested, as illustrated below; the "individual items" approach is usually used.

Thus, the entry to record the ending inventory data in Illustration 8–1 is usually made as follows:

a. Assuming periodic inventory procedures:

Inventory	71,000	
Loss on inventory reduction to market ($71,000 − $67,500)	3,500	
Income summary (or cost of goods sold)		71,000
Allowance for inventory reduction to market		3,500

b. Assuming perpetual inventory procedures:

Loss on inventory reduction to market	3,500	
Allowance for inventory reduction to market		3,500

Loss on Inventory Reduction to Market is usually added to the cost of goods sold on the income statement, and the Allowance for Inventory Reduction to Market is deducted from the related inventory on the balance sheet.

Illustration 8–1

| Commodity | Cost | Market | Lower of Cost or Market Applied to— | | |
			Individual Items	Major Classification	Total
Classification A:					
Item 1	$10,000	$ 9,500	$ 9,500		
Item 2	8,000	9,000	8,000		
	18,000	18,500		$18,000	
Classification B:					
Item 3	21,000	22,000	21,000		
Item 4	32,000	29,000	29,000		
	53,000	51,000		51,000	
Total	$71,000	$69,500			$69,500
Inventory Valuation . . .			$67,500	$69,000	$69,500

For purposes of determining an inventory *market* value (i.e., replacement cost) that may be lower than historical cost, this *market* value must fall within certain limits. The upper limit, or *ceiling,* is net realizable value, or selling price less costs of disposal. The lower limit, or *floor,* is net realizable value (i.e., ceiling) less a normal profit margin on the ordinary sale of the inventory item in question. If the replacement cost of the item exceeds the ceiling, this ceiling value is used as market. On the lower side, if the replacement cost is less than the floor value, the floor is used as market. Once *market* is so determined, market is compared to cost, and the lower (cost or market) is used to value the inventory.

Purchase Discounts

Cash discounts, whether taken or not upon payment of invoices, theoretically should be treated as reductions in the cost of the merchandise purchased; discounts not taken (lost) represent an interest charge. Therefore, a purchase of goods invoiced at $1,000, with terms 2/10, n/30 should be recorded as follows (at net):

```
Purchases (or inventory) . . . . . . . . . . . . . . . . . . .    980
    Accounts payable . . . . . . . . . . . . . . . . . . . . .           980
```

The entry for payment *within* the discount period would be:

```
Accounts payable . . . . . . . . . . . . . . . . . . . . . . .    980
    Cash  . . . . . . . . . . . . . . . . . . . . . . . . . . .           980
```

The entry for payment *after* the discount period would be:

```
Accounts payable . . . . . . . . . . . . . . . . . . . . . . .    980
Interest expense  . . . . . . . . . . . . . . . . . . . . . . .     20
    Cash  . . . . . . . . . . . . . . . . . . . . . . . . . . .         1,000
```

If payment after the discount period is anticipated in a later accounting period, correct accounting would require the following *adjusting entry* at the end of the accounting period in which the purchase was made:

```
Interest expense  . . . . . . . . . . . . . . . . . . . . . . .     20
    Estimated liability for purchase discounts lost (a current liability)  . .      20
```

Because of precedent, and for practical reasons, purchase discounts frequently are accounted for in a theoretically incorrect way, as follows (at gross):

Answer frame 1[8]

1. False. Inventories are classified as current assets regardless of the nature of the inventory. For example, the *inventory* of a construction company may be houses or other structures which, if they were *not inventory,* would be classified as operational assets.
2. False. Both methods produce the same net income. But the perpetual system provides for a *continuous* record of inventory on hand; the periodic system does not.
3. True. This pair of statements reflects the essence of inventory accounting under the periodic system. See the illustrative entries in this frame for elaboration.
4. True. Beginning Inventory + Purchases − Ending Inventory = Cost of Goods Sold. If the values of any three of the above variables are known, we can solve for the fourth variable. In this case, Beginning Inventory + $20,000 − $6,000 = $30,000. Therefore, beginning inventory *must be* $16,000.
5. True. Only errors involving ending inventory (beginning inventory for the next year) affect two years' reported net incomes.

If you missed any of the above, reread Frame 1[8] before beginning Frame 2[8], page 62.

Frame 2[8] continued

a. To record the purchase:

Purchases (or inventory)	1,000	
Accounts payable		1,000

b. To record payment *within* the discount period:

Accounts payable	1,000	
Cash		980
Purchase discounts		20

c. To record payment *after* the discount period:

Accounts payable	1,000	
Cash		1,000

Relative Sales Value Method of Cost Allocation

When different inventory items are purchased for a flat price and then sorted into different categories, it is necessary to record the purchase price of each category separately in the inventory records. A common method of allocating the lump-sum price in such a purchase is the *relative sales value* method; that is, the lump-sum cost is allocated on the basis of the weighted relative sales values of the several categories of inventory.

To illustrate, assume the purchase of two separate tracts of land for a lump-sum cost of $125,000. Pursuant to negotiating a price, the purchaser commissioned a real estate appraiser to appraise the land. This expert believed the tracts to be worth $75,000 and $60,000. (As a matter of fact, the seller was willing to sell the land at a "bargain" because he had an immediate need for cash.) Therefore, the problem exists as to how to prorate the cost of $125,000 to two tracts worth a total of $135,000. The relative-sales-value (RSV) method is used as follows:

	Market Value	*Fraction of Total Sales Value*		*Cost*	*Prorated Cost*
Tract A	$ 75,000	$75,000/$135,000	×	$125,000	$ 69,444
Tract B	60,000	$60,000/$135,000	×	$125,000	55,556
Total	$135,000				$125,000

Therefore, the entry to record the acquisition of the land is:

```
Land—Tract A . . . . . . . . . . . . . . . . . . . . . .    69,444
Land—Tract B . . . . . . . . . . . . . . . . . . . . . .    55,556
    Cash   . . . . . . . . . . . . . . . . . . . . . . .              125,000
```

Is each of the following statements true or false?

———— 1. Application of the lower-of-cost-or-market (LCM) valuation to individual items of inventory *always* produces a lower inventory value than application of LCM to the entire inventory as a unit.

———— 2. Use of net realizable value as the ceiling in determination of "market" (pursuant to valuing inventories at the lower of cost or market) is theoretically sound because it does not make sense to *ever* value inventory at greater than its current net selling price, given the historical cost framework.

———— 3. Recording inventory purchases net of discount is consistent with valuing assets at the *present value* of the future cash flows necessary to acquire the assets (inventory in this case).

———— 4. The relative sales value (RSV) method represents a departure from the cost principle.

Now compare your answers with those given in Answer Frame 2[8], page 66.

Answer frame 2⁸

1. False. LCM applied to individual items and LCM applied to the entire inventory as a unit will produce identical LCM valuations when (*a*) cost and market are the same for every item, (*b*) cost is lower than market for every item, *or* (*c*) cost exceeds market for every item. In general, however, market will exceed cost for *most* items, whereas cost will exceed market for a *few* items. In this case applications of LCM to individual items will produce a lower inventory valuation than application of LCM to the entire inventory as a whole. In no case will application of LCM to the entire inventory produce a *lower* valuation than LCM applied to individual items.

2. True. This statement represents sound reasoning.

3. True. The *discount* offered for timely payment is in fact interest on the *present value* of the amount payable for the inventory. In general, we value assets acquired on credit at the present value of the debt, and in this sense, so valuing inventory is consistent with valuing inventory on a present value basis.

4. Not necessarily. The RSV method is simply a method of *proration*. If proration of *cost* is the intended use of the RSV method, then the method does not involve a departure from the cost principle. In fact, the RSV method is used most often in accounting to prorate *cost* to individual items for which individual costs are not explicitly given.

If you missed any of the above questions, you should reread Frame 2⁸ before proceeding. Then continue reading with Chapter 9.

chapter 9

INVENTORIES—FLOW AND MATCHING PROCEDURES

Frame 1[9]

Inventory Flow Procedures

In Chapter 8 it was noted that one of the important problems in accounting for inventories is the selection of an appropriate *inventory cost flow method,* such as Fifo, Lifo, and so forth. This problem arises when units of inventory are purchased at different unit costs. Selection of an appropriate unit cost for units sold (cost of goods sold) and for units on hand (inventory) on a consistent basis necessitates the establishment of a definite inventory cost flow policy by the management of the firm. This chapter considers the following commonly used inventory flow methods: specific cost; average cost; first-in, first-out (Fifo); last-in, first-out (Lifo); and some complications in applying Lifo. For purposes of illustration, the following purchases, sales, and inventory data are used:

	Transactions	Received Units	Received Unit Cost	Units Issued	Units on Hand
Jan. 1	Inventory (@ $1)				200
9	Purchase	300	$1.10		500
10	Sale			400	100
15	Purchase	400	1.16		500
18	Sale			300	200
24	Purchase	100	1.26		300

From the above data we can focus on the inventory flow problem as follows:

Goods available for sale (issue):	Units	Unit Cost	Total Cost
Jan. 1 Inventory	200	$1.00	$ 200.00
9 Purchase	300	1.10	330.00
15 Purchase	400	1.16	464.00
24 Purchase	100	1.26	126.00
Total goods available for sale (issue)	1,000		$1,120.00
Less: Final inventory	300		?
Difference: Cost of Goods Sold (Issued)	700		$?

The application of the several inventory flow methods and the related accounting entries will vary somewhat depending on whether *periodic* inventory procedures (physical count) or *perpetual* inventory pro-

67

cedures (continuous inventory record) are utilized. Each flow method will be considered in the order listed above.

Specific Cost.   When the individual items in inventory have unique characteristics and small quantities are involved, it may be feasible to tag or number each unit when purchased or manufactured so that the actual unit cost is known for each unit of the item; thus it is possible to readily identify the unit cost for each issue (sale) and also for each unit of the item included in the inventory. The specific cost method identifies the *cost flow* precisely with the *physical flow* of the goods. It is used infrequently because of the clerical requirements; there is also the possibility of profit manipulation by arbitrary selection of the items for cost flow purposes. However, for *unique* items of inventory such as jewels or houses, specific cost should be used.

Average Cost.   There are two acceptable variations of this method; the weighted average unit cost and the moving average unit cost. The *weighted average* cost per unit is determined at the end of the period, based upon the beginning inventory plus all purchases. To illustrate, utilizing the data given above:

	Units	Total Cost
Total goods available for sale	1,000	$1,120.00
Weighted average unit cost ($1,120.00 ÷ 1,000 units) = $1.12 .		
Valuation of final inventory (300 @ $1.12)	300 × $1.12 =	336.00
Difference: Cost of Goods Sold (Issued)	700 × $1.12 =	$ 784.00

The weighted average approach is seldom used with perpetual inventory procedures since the average unit cost cannot be computed until the end of the period. The method is theoretically and mathematically sound. It is easy to understand and apply, and it is widely used with *periodic* inventory procedures.

The *moving average* is commonly applied with perpetual inventory procedures since it provides an average unit cost developed throughout the period; it involves the computation of a new average after each receipt (purchase) of goods. This is shown in Illustration 9–1.

Illustration 9–1

Perpetual Inventory Record (moving average illustrated)

Date	Received			Issued			Balance		
	Units	Unit Cost	Total Cost	Units	Unit Cost	Total Cost	Units	Unit Cost	Total Cost
Jan. 1							200	$1.00	$200
9	300	$1.10	$330				500	1.06*	530
10				400	$1.06	$424	100	1.06	106
15	400	1.16	464				500	1.14*	570
18				300	1.14	342	200	1.14	228
24	100	1.26	126				300	1.18*	354

* New average computed; for example, $530 ÷ 500 units = $1.06.

First-In, First-Out.   This method rests upon the flow-of-cost assumption that upon sale (issue) of goods, the unit cost should flow out in the same order that the costs flowed in; as a consequence, issues are first costed out at the oldest unit costs and the remaining inventory is costed at the *most recent* unit costs. To illustrate, utilizing the data given above:

	Units	Total Cost
Total goods available for sale	1,000	$1,120

ENDING
INVENTORY
COMPUTATION

Valuation of final inventory (Fifo):
100 units @ $1.26 (most recent
purchase) $126
200 units @ $1.16 (next most recent
purchase) 232

	Units	Total Cost
Total inventory	300	358
Difference: Cost of Goods Sold (Issued)	700	$ 762

The Fifo method is equally adaptable for periodic inventory (illustrated above) and perpetual inventory procedures (Illustration 9–2). Fifo is widely used since (*a*) it is adaptable for either periodic or perpetual

Illustration 9–2

Perpetual Inventory Record (Fifo illustrated)

Date	Received			Issued			Balance		
	Units	Unit Cost	Total Cost	Units	Unit Cost	Total Cost	Units	Unit Cost	Total Cost
Jan. 1							200	$1.00	$200
9	300	$1.10	$330				200	1.00	200
							300	1.10	330
10				200	$1.00	$200			
				200	1.10	220	100	1.10	110
15	400	1.16	464				100	1.10	110
							400	1.16	464
18				100	1.10	110			
				200	1.16	232	200	1.16	232
24	100	1.26	126				200	1.16	232 ⎫
							100	1.26	126 ⎬
									$358

inventory procedures; (*b*) it produces an inventory valuation which approximates current replacement cost; and (*c*) it is relatively easy to apply.

Last-In, First-Out. This method is based upon the flow of cost assumption that current inventory acquisition costs are largely, if not wholly, incurred for the purpose of meeting current sales or manufacturing requirements and, as a consequence, that the latest costs should be charged against current sales. Under this method the cost of the units remaining in inventory represents the *oldest* cost available.

Lifo may be applied under either periodic or perpetual inventory procedures. Using the illustrative data given above, Lifo costs would be assigned at the end of the period to a *periodic* inventory system as follows:

INVENTORY
COMPUTATION

Goods available $1,120
Deduct final inventory (300 units per physical inventory count):
200 units @ $1 (oldest costs available, from January 1 inventory) $200
100 units @ $1.10 (next oldest costs available, from January 9 purchase) 110

Total inventory 310

Cost of Sales (or Issues) . . . . $ 810

When Lifo is applied to *perpetual* inventory procedures, the *issues* usually are costed in the perpetual inventory records *currently* throughout the period. The application of Lifo under perpetual inventory procedures is shown in Illustration 9–3; note the maintenance of "inventory layers" for each different unit cost in the Balance column.

Illustration 9–3

Perpetual Inventory Record (Lifo illustrated—costed currently)

Date	Received			Issued or Sold			Balance		
	Units	Unit Cost	Total Cost	Units	Unit Cost	Total Cost	Units	Unit Cost	Total Cost
Jan. 1							200	$1.00	$200
9	300	$1.10	$330				200	1.00	200
							300	1.10	330
10				300	$1.10	$330			
				100	1.00	100	100	1.00	100
15	400	1.16	464				100	1.00	100
							400	1.16	464
18				300	1.16	348	100	1.00	100
							100	1.16·	116
24	100	1.26	126				100	1.00	100 ⎫
							100	1.16	116 ⎬
							100	1.26	126 ⎭
									$342

It should be noted that in the two Lifo illustrations the inventory valuation is different by $32 ($310 versus $342) due to the fact that the pricing of issues at the *end* of the period (periodic inventory procedure) compared with pricing the issues *during* the period (perpetual inventory procedure) may leave different layers in the final inventory.

Indicate whether each statement below is true or false.

———— 1. In general, Fifo will produce the highest ending inventory cost, the average method the next highest and Lifo the lowest inventory cost— as long as inventory unit costs are rising.

———— 2. With rising prices and a high level of purchases and sales activity, the weighted average cost method will produce an ending inventory balance that is *greater than* the ending inventory balance under the moving average method.

———— 3. Perpetual inventory procedures involve a greater cost to maintain than a periodic system does.

———— 4. Fifo and Lifo represent fundamentally different conceptual approaches to asset valuation and income measurement.

Now refer to Answer Frame 1⁹, page 72.

Frame 2⁹ ——————————————————————————

Unique Aspects of Lifo

Lifo is designed to match *current* cost (of goods sold) against *current* revenue. Of course, Lifo also produces lower reported profits than the other methods—as long as prices are rising. Therefore, to the extent that Lifo is used for *income tax* purposes (as distinguished from *financial accounting* purposes), Lifo saves a corporation cash via lower income taxes. This reveals an interesting paradox: The company which uses Fifo *reports* the higher profits, but the company which uses Lifo has more cash, other things equal.

Because of this paradoxical situation (and other related factors) the Internal Revenue Service requires companies to use Lifo for income tax purposes only if they also use Lifo for financial reporting (to their stockholders). Therefore, a company must use Lifo for financial accounting purposes as a condition for being allowed to use Lifo for tax purposes. (Specific cost, Fifo, and average cost methods are also acceptable for tax purposes.)

Complications in Applying Lifo

Specific identification, Fifo, and average cost methods generally give rise to no special accounting problems other than the general tedium associated with the accounting function. Lifo cost, on the other hand, does present unique accounting problems because of the conceptual nature of Lifo. For example, the keystone of Lifo is the matching of reasonably current (i.e., last-in) cost of inventory against revenue. This, of course, means that the ending inventory cost consists of the older (i.e., first-in) costs. One problem in applying Lifo involves the question: How *old* should those costs of ending inventory be? Theoretically, ending inventory could contain the *cost* of inventory that was purchased when the company began its operations—perhaps 20, 50, or 100 years earlier. The general notion involved in this question is that under Lifo the company permanently keeps a *base layer* of inventory, that is, the base layer of inventory is *not* sold (i.e., liquidated).

Lifo Inventory Liquidation

When a company fails to maintain the normal, or "base," inventory position, a special problem is created under Lifo. The problem is that liquidation (i.e., sale) of the base layer of inventory forces the company to "cost" these sales at the lower cost of the base layer, which increases reported net income. This effect of higher reported profits on these sales is contrary to the theoretical foundation of Lifo, namely, matching *current* cost of inventory (for units sold) against *current* revenue. To illustrate assume the following:

	Units	Unit Cost	Total Cost
Beginning inventory (assumed to be the base layer of inventory) . .	10,000	$1.00	$10,000
Purchases	40,000	1.50	60,000
Total available for sale . .	50,000		70,000
Sales (45,000 units, issues on Lifo basis) {	40,000	1.50	60,000
	5,000	1.00	5,000
	45,000		65,000
Final Inventory	5,000	1.00	$ 5,000

In the above example the company failed to maintain the base inventory level—by 5,000 units. When the inventory liquidation is considered *temporary,* the cost of goods sold (issues) should be charged with replacement cost (assumed to be $1.60); the inventory account should be credited at Lifo cost, and the difference credited to a special liability account as follows:

Cost of goods sold (40,000 @ $1.50) + (5,000 @ $1.60) 68,000
 Inventory (per sales above)   65,000
 Excess of replacement cost over cost of inventory temporarily
  liquidated* [5,000 × ($1.60 − $1.00)]   3,000
   * A current liability account.

Answer frame 1⁹

1. True. This is clear from the examples used in this frame. Refer once again, if necessary, to the basic data (given on page 67) used for all the examples. Note in particular that inventory costs are rising—from $1 to $1.26. Also note that ending inventory under:

Fifo—whether costed currently or at the end of the period (page 69) $358
Weighted average cost (page 68) 336
Lifo—applied at the end of the period, to *periodic* inventory systems (page 69) . . 310

Fifo—whether costed currently or at the end of the period (page 69) $358
Moving average cost (page 68) 354
Lifo—applied currently during the period, to *perpetual* inventory systems (page 70) 342

2. False. The reverse is true. That is, given rising prices and high volume, moving average cost will exceed weighted average cost because the weighted *average* averages across all unit costs of the period—including the lower unit cost of items in beginning inventory. By contrast, the moving average cost only includes the more recent unit costs. This is because of the *nature* of the *moving* average. For evidence of the validity of this answer, examine the difference between weighted average cost ($336) and moving average cost ($354) presented in the answer given above to question 1.

3. True. This is one appealing feature—lower accounting costs—of the periodic system. But the perpetual system is absolutely necessary in many cases.

4. True. Fifo emphasizes the balance sheet by assigning the more recent unit costs to ending inventory (which is reported on the balance sheet) whereas Lifo emphasizes the income statement by assigning the more recent unit costs to cost of goods sold (which is an expense and hence reported on the income statement).

If you missed any of the above, reread Frame 1⁹ before beginning Frame 2⁹, page 70.

Frame 2⁹ continued

When the liquidated inventory is replaced (base layer restored) the following entry is made:

Inventory (5,000 @ $1) 5,000
Excess of replacement cost over cost of inventory temporarily liquidated*
    (5,000 @ $.60) 3,000
        Accounts payable (5,000 @ $1.60)   8,000
        * A current liability account.

Dollar-Value Lifo

Even though it was not emphasized above, all the inventory costing methods covered thus far employ a "quantity-of-goods" orientation. That is, the manner of arriving at ending inventory each period has involved determination of (*a*) the quantity of goods on hand—from a physical count and/or the perpetual inventory records and (*b*) the appropriate cost per unit, based on specific cost, Fifo cost, average cost, *or* Lifo cost. In all cases the focus was placed on the *quantity* of goods.

Imagine for the moment a large corporation that has several hundred different types of finished goods in inventory and that these different products were added to the company's operations at many different times. It is clear that accounting for this company's inventories is a very complex task—under any costing method. However, the complexities become particularly onerous under Lifo because of the very nature of Lifo.

Methods of dealing with the inherent complexity of Lifo have been devised. The remainder of this frame covers one such approach, and it is known as *dollar-value Lifo*. As the name implies, the method applies Lifo, but to *dollars* of inventory cost rather than to units of inventory. Thus, the standard inventory accounting unit in a dollar-value Lifo context is the *dollar*. Use of the dollar as the basic inventory unit enables a company to aggregate across "similar," but not identical, types of inventory. The aggregate groups of *dollars* of inventory are known as "pools." Therefore, the hypothetical corporation mentioned above may be able to synthesize its 200 products into four or five natural business units, or pools, and greatly simplify its inventory accounting (and the related cost of processing the information). In addition to being cost efficient, the dollar-value-Lifo method is also conceptually sound.[1]

Proper application of any Lifo method requires that different cost layers be accorded separate treatment. Dollar-value Lifo is no exception. Under dollar-value Lifo, the separate treatment accorded inventory layers acquired at different costs involves the use of ratios, or indexes, of current-year costs to base-year costs.

Dollar-value Lifo procedures involve five distinct steps that may be divided into two different phases, summarized as follows:

Phase A—Computation of an internal index for the current year that is specific to the inventory pool:

Step 1. Determine the base year inventory in dollars; that is, the inventory value at the date of adoption of Lifo. This base inventory is maintained permanently if at all possible.

Step 2. As the denominator for the index calculation, cost the ending inventory for the current period *at base year costs*.

Step 3. As the numerator for the index calculation, cost the ending inventory for the current period at *current year costs*.

Step 4. Compute the internal price index ratio for the current year by dividing the results of Step 3 by Step 2.

Phase B—Computation of Lifo inventory by application of index numbers:

Step 5. Convert the ending inventory layers, priced at base year costs, to the ending inventory layers at Lifo cost by applying the index number applicable to each layer.

To illustrate dollar-value Lifo computations, suppose that MR, Inc., sells two different items, A and B, which are similar. The company used Fifo through 19A. Starting in 19B, Lifo was adopted for both book and tax purposes. The company's purchases and sales activity for 19B and 19C are as follows:

Inventory Data per Accounts (Fifo basis)

	Item A			Item B			Total Amount (Items A & B)
	Units	Cost	Total	Units	Cost	Total	
Year 19A:							
Ending inventory under Fifo:							
Layer 1	1,000	$1.00	$1,000	2,000	$2.00	$ 4,000	
Layer 2				500	2.20	1,100	
	1,000	$1.00	$1,000	2,500	$2.04	$ 5,100	$6,100
Year 19B:							
Purchases	3,000	$1.20	$3,600	4,000	$2.50	$10,000	
Sales	(2,800)			(3,500)			
Ending inventory under Fifo:	1,200	1.20	1,440	3,000	2.50	7,500	$8,940
Year 19C:							
Purchases	3,300	1.30	4,290	4,200	2.60	10,920	
Sales	(3,200)			(4,200)			
Ending inventory under Fifo:	1,300	1.30	1,690	3,000	2.60	7,800	$9,490

---

[1] There are two ways of applying dollar-value Lifo: double extension and link chain. Because the two methods are quite similar, only double extension is covered in this book. Also, double extension is a little simpler computationally as well.

The problem is to compute the ending inventories on the dollar-value Lifo method for 19B and 19C. The solution applies the five steps given above and proceeds as follows:

Phase A—Computation of Internal Index for Current Year

Step 1. Base inventory when Lifo adopted (at base year costs):
Beginning of base year (19B):

Item A	1,000 @ $1.00	$1,000
Item B	2,500 2.04	5,100
Total Base Inventory		$6,100

Step 2. Ending inventory at base year costs:

	Year End 19B		Year End 19C	
Item A	1,200 @ $1.00 $1,200		1,300 @ $1.00 $1,300	
Item B	3,000 2.04 6,120		3,000 2.04 6,120	
Total Ending Inventory at Base Year Costs	$7,320		$7,420	

Step 3. Ending inventory at current year costs:

Item A	1,200 @ $1.20	$1,440
Item B	3,000 2.50	7,500
19B—Total Ending Inventory at Current Costs		$8,940

Item A	1,300 @ $1.30	$1,690
Item B	3,000 2.60	7,800
19C—Total Ending Inventory at Current Costs		$9,490

Step 4. Current year index:
Current Year Costs ÷ Base Year Costs:

	19B	19C
19B $8,940 ÷ $7,320	1.221	
19C $9,490 ÷ $7,420		1.279

Phase B—Computation of Ending Lifo Inventory Amount

	Ending Inventory at Base Year Costs	Index (from Step 4)	Ending Inventory at Lifo Cost
Step 5.			
End of 19B:			
Base year beginning inventory	$6,100	1.000	$6,100
Incremental layer: 19B ($7,320 − $6,100)	1,220	1.221	1,490
Ending inventory at Lifo	$7,320		$7,590
End of 19C:			
Base year beginning inventory	$6,100	1.000	$6,100
Incremental layers: 19B (from 19B)	1,220	1.221	1,490
19C ($7,420 − $7,320)	100	1.279	128
Ending Inventory at Lifo	$7,420		$7,718

In conclusion, two general principles of applying dollar-value Lifo are:

1. Cost each layer of inventory at the index for the year when the layer was added. If all or part of the base layer of inventory is liquidated and later replaced, the replacement layer should be added at the index for the year of replacement, not at the base year index. Effectively you create a newly composed base layer. The same principle applies to the liquidation and replacement of a layer other than the base layer.
2. Account for layers that are liquidated in reverse order from the order in which they were acquired. This principle is implicit in the general Lifo approach.

In conclusion, the foregoing discussion of dollar-value Lifo has been concerned with the year-end determination of ending inventory, which of course is one of the three separate elements in cost of goods sold. Therefore, if *beginning inventory* at dollar-value Lifo is $10,000, purchases for the period total $35,000, and *ending inventory* at dollar-value Lifo (the focus in this discussion) is $12,500, cost of goods sold for the period is $32,500 ($10,000 + $35,000 − $12,500). Then the process will repeat itself in the next accounting period, starting with beginning inventory of $12,500 at dollar-value Lifo, and so forth.

True or false?

———— 1. Inventory liquidation is an accounting problem that is unique to the Lifo method.

———— 2. The purpose of costing a liquidated base layer of inventory (accounted for on the dollar-value Lifo method) at replacement cost is to maintain the integrity of Lifo in the determination of cost of goods sold.

Now work the following problems on the dollar-value Lifo inventory method.

3. Compute MR, Inc.'s ending inventory balance at dollar-value Lifo for 19B, 19C, and 19D, using the Fifo data given below:

		Purchases			Issues			Balance		
								Records Pertain to Ten Products		
19A:	Ending inventory (at Fifo) . .							400	$1.00	$400
19B:	Purchase . . .	700	$1.20	$840				400	1.00	400
								700	1.20	840
	Sale (@ $3.00)				400	$1.00	$400			
					100	1.20	120	600	1.20	720
19C:	Purchase . . .	600	1.35	810				600	1.20	720
								600	1.35	810
	Sale (@ $3.40)				600	1.20	720			
					200	1.35	270	400	1.35	540
19D:	Purchase . . .	500	1.50	750				400	1.35	540
								500	1.50	750
	Sale (@ $3.75)				400	1.35	540	500	1.50	750

Note: When dollar-value Lifo is initially adopted, it is necessary to begin with base year inventory (i.e., beginning inventory for the year of adoption) stated at *Fifo* cost. This accomplishes the purpose of having the base year inventory stated at reasonably current costs—as of the time when dollar-value Lifo was adopted.

4. Same as Question 3 above, but let ending inventory quantities for 19B, 19C, and 19D, respectively, be 400, 300, and 500. Compute ending inventory costs on the dollar-value Lifo method for the three years.

Now compare your answers with those given in Answer Frame 2[9], page 76.

Answer frame 2⁹

1. True. Liquidation problems are unique to Lifo because Lifo is the only inventory method for which the *base layer* concept is important.
2. True. This statement reflects sound reasoning in regard to Lifo, whether it is dollar-value Lifo or quantity-of-goods Lifo.
3. Ending inventory, under dollar-value Lifo, for 19B is $640; for 19C it is $400; and for 19D it is $550. Computations are as follows:

    Steps 1–4 outlined in the general dollar-value Lifo solution are combined to determine the respective year index values:

	19B	19C	19D
Ending inventory at current cost	600 @ $1.20	400 @ $1.35	500 @ $1.50
Ending inventory at base year cost	600 @ $1.00 = 1.20	400 @ $1.00 = 1.35	500 @ $1.00 = 1.50

    Step 5—Compute ending inventory:

	19B	19C	19D
Base layer of inventory: 400 × $1	$400	$400	$400
Additional layers: 19B ($600 − $400) × 1.20	240		
19D ($500 − $400) × 1.50			150
	$640	$400	$550

4. Indexes are 1.20, 1.35, and 1.50 for 19B, 19C and 19D, respectively. Ending inventories at dollar-value Lifo for the three years are $400, $300, and $600, computed as follows:

	19B	19C	19D
Base layer of inventory—19B: 400 × $1	$400		
Base layer of inventory—19C and 19D: 300 × $1		$300	$300
Additional layer: 19D ($500 − $300) × 1.50			300
	$400	$300	$600

If you missed any of the above questions, you should reread Frame 2⁹ before proceeding. Then continue reading with Chapter 10.

chapter 10

INVENTORIES—SPECIAL
VALUATION PROCEDURES

Frame 1[10]

Estimating Inventories

There are numerous situations where the accountant, due to the unavailability of actual data, must be concerned with estimating the final inventory. As a result certain inventory estimation procedures are widely utilized. The principal procedures are the gross margin (profit) method and the retail inventory method.

Gross Margin Method. This represents an approach frequently utilized to approximate the valuation of the inventory independently of a physical count of the goods; it is also frequently used as a "check" on an inventory valuation derived in the usual manner (periodic or perpetual). The method is based upon the assumption that in the short run the rate of gross margin (gross margin divided by sales) is approximately the same from one accounting period to the next. To apply the gross margin method, certain basic data must be known, namely sales, goods available for sale, and an estimate of the gross margin rate. To illustrate assume the following data are available:

1. Actual amounts (from the accounting records):

    Sales, net of returns and discounts $5,000

    Goods available for sale:
    Beginning inventory 2,500
    Purchases, including freight-in and net of returns and discounts . . 3,500

2. Estimated amount:

    Gross margin rate, stated as a percent of sales 20%

The valuation of the final inventory may be *estimated* as follows:

Goods available for sale:
Beginning inventory $2,500
Add: Purchases 3,500
        Goods available for sale $6,000

Deduct sales reduced to estimated cost:
Sales 5,000
    Less: Estimated gross margin ($5,000 × 20%)   1,000
Estimated cost of goods sold   4,000
Difference: Estimated Cost of Final Inventory . $2,000

The gross margin method of estimating the final inventory frequently is employed in a number of different situations, for example,

1.   By auditors to test the overall *reasonableness* of an inventory valuation that was determined by other means.
2.   To estimate the final inventory for monthly financial statements when it is not feasible to take a physical inventory.
3.   To estimate the value of an inventory destroyed by a casualty, such as fire or flood.
4.   To develop budget estimates of inventories for planning purposes.

In applying the method it must be kept in mind that the resultant inventory valuation is no more accurate than the gross margin rate, which is both an *average* rate and an *estimated* rate.

Retail Inventory Method.   This method is widely employed by retail stores which sell a variety of items. In such situations perpetual inventory procedures are both costly and time consuming and therefore not efficient. As a consequence, for interim (monthly or quarterly) financial statements some method of *estimating* the final inventory must be utilized. Several features of department store operation make possible the utilization of the retail inventory method. Particular features are (*a*) each department tends to be homogeneous with respect to the percent of markup on all items stocked in the department and (*b*) articles purchased are immediately priced at retail and shelved. The retail method of estimating inventory is similar in some respects to the gross margin method explained above, but instead of estimating a gross margin rate, the retail method utilizes an *average single-period ratio* of cost to retail. Determination of the cost ratio and its use for computing the ending inventory is illustrated below with simplified data:

	At Cost	At Retail
Goods available for sale:		
Beginning inventory (January 1)	$ 15,000*	$ 25,000*
Purchases during January	195,000*	275,000*
Cost of goods available for sale . . .	$210.000	300,000
Cost ratio: ($210,000 ÷ $300,000 = 70%) . .		
Deduct January sales at retail		260,000*
Ending inventory (January 31):		
At retail		$ 40,000
At cost ($40,000 × 70%)	$ 28.000	

* Data provided by the accounting records.

Note in the above example that the *cost ratio* is computed by dividing the goods available for sale *at cost* by the goods available for sale *at retail;* the cost ratio then is used to restate the ending inventory at cost ($28,000 in the above illustration) which would be shown as the final inventory in the financial statements. Note also in the example that the accounting records must be maintained so as to provide actual data for *five* different amounts (noted above with asterisks).

Markups and Markdowns.   In the above illustration it was assumed that there were no changes in the *original* marked selling prices; that is, it was assumed that there were no *additional* markups or any markdowns. In addition to the data indicated above, the retail inventory method requires that a precise record of the *amount* of all *additional markups* and *markdowns* be maintained in the accounting records since these two items will affect both the cost ratio and the final inventory valuation. Thus, to apply the retail inventory method a careful distinction must be maintained between the following: markup, additional markups, markup cancellations, markdowns, and markdown cancellations. To illustrate, assume:

1.   An item is purchased for $1.50 and marked originally to sell for $2 and placed on the shelf; there has been a *markup* of $.50.
2.   Now assume the article prior to sale is remarked to sell at $2.25; now there is a *markup* of $.50 and an *additional markup* of $.25.

3. Now assume the article did not sell and is again remarked, but at $1.90; now there is a *markup* of $.50, and an *additional markup* of $.25, a *markup cancellation* of $.25, and a *markdown* of $.10. Note that the *original* marked price of $2 (rather than cost) is the base point in these definitions of the markdown.

To illustrate the retail inventory method in a more complex situation, where additional markups and markdowns are involved, assume the accounting records provide the following data:

	At Cost	At Retail
Inventory at beginning of period	$ 550	$ 900
Purchases during period	6,290	9,400
Additional markups during period		225
Markup cancellations during period		25
Markdowns during period		600
Markdown cancellations during period		100
Sales for the period		8,500

To compute the final inventory utilizing the above data:

Retail Inventory Method—Estimating Average Cost

		At Cost	At Retail
Goods available for sale:			
Beginning inventory		$ 550*	$ 900*
Purchases during period		6,290*	9,400*
Additional markups	$225*		
Less: Markup cancellations	25*		
Net additional markups			200
Markdowns	(600)*		
Less: Markdown cancellations	100*		
Net markdowns			(500)
Goods available for sale		$6.840	10,000
Cost ratio: ($6,840 ÷ $10,000 = 68.4%)			
Deduct:			
Sales			8,500*
Ending inventory:			
At retail			$ 1,500
At cost ($1,500 × 68.4%)		$1.026	

* Data provided by accounting records.

The cost ratio (of 68.4%) in this example reflected an *average* comprising both the beginning inventory and the purchases during the period. Thus, the example is appropriately labeled above as applying to the retail method of estimating *average cost*.

The retail method can also be used to estimate:

a. Fifo cost.
b. Lower of cost (Fifo or average) or market (abbreviated as LCM).

The modifications that are needed in the above computations in order to accommodate Fifo and LCM are straightforward. For example, given the above data, ending inventory at Fifo cost as estimated by the retail method would be $1,037. The only modifications in the above computations are:

1. Fifo cost ratio is 69.1%, which is the ratio of purchases at cost ($6,290) *to* the sum of (*a*) purchases at retail ($9,400), (*b*) net additional markups ($200), and (*c*) net markdowns (negative $500). Thus, $6,290 ÷ $9,100 = 69.1%. This modification, though somewhat arbitrary, is consistent with the definition of Fifo in that it excludes beginning inventory from the determination of the cost ratio.
2. Application of the Fifo cost ratio (69.1%) to ending inventory at retail ($1,500). Thus, estimated Fifo inventory per the retail method is $1,037 ($1,500 × 69.1%).

The modification needed for estimating LCM for a retail inventory involves excluding net markdowns from the computation of the cost ratio. This exclusion produces a lower cost ratio, which in turn produces a lower inventory valuation, and this is consistent with LCM. Using the data above, we estimate the lower of *average* cost or market of the ending inventory to be $977. The cost ratio is 65.1% [$6,840 ÷ ($900 + $9,400 + $200)], and the ending inventory at the lower of average cost or market is $977 ($1,500 × 65.1%). Alternatively, the lower of *Fifo* cost or market of the ending inventory is $983. The cost ratio is 65.5% [$6,290 ÷ ($9,400 + $200)], and the ending inventory is estimated at the lower of Fifo cost or market to be $983 ($1,500 × 65.5%).

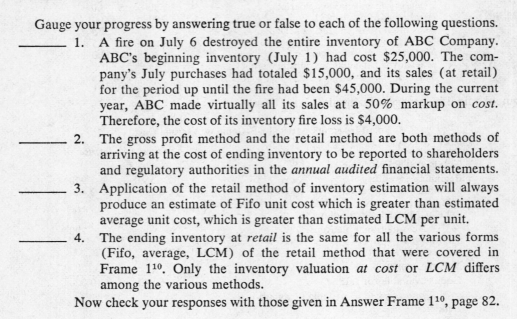

Gauge your progress by answering true or false to each of the following questions.

_____ 1.   A fire on July 6 destroyed the entire inventory of ABC Company. ABC's beginning inventory (July 1) had cost $25,000. The company's July purchases had totaled $15,000, and its sales (at retail) for the period up until the fire had been $45,000. During the current year, ABC made virtually all its sales at a 50% markup on *cost.* Therefore, the cost of its inventory fire loss is $4,000.

_____ 2.   The gross profit method and the retail method are both methods of arriving at the cost of ending inventory to be reported to shareholders and regulatory authorities in the *annual audited* financial statements.

_____ 3.   Application of the retail method of inventory estimation will always produce an estimate of Fifo unit cost which is greater than estimated average unit cost, which is greater than estimated LCM per unit.

_____ 4.   The ending inventory at *retail* is the same for all the various forms (Fifo, average, LCM) of the retail method that were covered in Frame 1[10]. Only the inventory valuation *at cost* or *LCM* differs among the various methods.

Now check your responses with those given in Answer Frame 1[10], page 82.

Frame 2[10]

Frame 1[10] covered the retail method of estimating inventory cost under Fifo cost, average cost, and LCM. The present frame covers the *retail-Lifo* method, as well as inventories (and income) on long-term construction contracts.

Retail Lifo Inventory Estimation

The *retail* method can also be modified to produce an estimate of the *Lifo* cost of ending inventory. The "retail-Lifo" method, as it is known, also utilizes the dollar-value Lifo concept that was discussed in Chapter 9. Basically, this involves the use of an inventory cost index in order to account for layers of inventory that are added to a base (Lifo) layer.

Computation of a retail-Lifo estimate of inventory cost can be accomplished in four steps:

1.   Computation or selection of an appropriate price index.
2.   Computation of the *cost-to-retail* ratio, per the Fifo method covered in Frame 1[10].
3.   Computation of the ending inventory, at *retail,* as covered in Frame 1[10].
4.   Computation of the ending inventory, at *Lifo* cost, by applying the index (step 1) to the ending inventory at retail (step 3).

To illustrate the retail-Lifo computations, assume the following basic data for WZ Company:

	19B		19C	
	At Cost	At Retail	At Cost	At Retail
Beginning (base) inventory	$17,400	$ 30,000		
Purchases	90,480	147,000	$101,500	$172,000
Net additional markups		8,800		9,000
Net markdowns		5,000		6,000
Sales		140,000		162,800
Applicable price index (19A = 100)		102		106

Assume the company has been using the dollar-value, retail-Lifo method for external reporting and income tax purposes. The company uses a published index selected from an external source. Computations of the ending inventories for 19B and 19C under the retail-Lifo method are given in Illustration 10–1.

Illustration 10–1. Computation of Inventory on Retail-Lifo Method

Step		19B			19C		
1. Price index computed or selected (19A = 100) .		102			106		
2. Computation of cost-to-retail ratio—per Fifo method:							
	At Cost	At Retail	Cost Ratio	At Cost	At Retail	Cost Ratio	
Inventory, January 1 . . .	$17,400	$ 30,000					
Purchases	90,480	147,000		$101,500	$172,000		
Net additional markups . .		8,800			9,000		
Net markdowns		(5,000)			(6,000)		
Total (excluding beginning inventory) . .	$90,480	150,800	.60	$101,500	175,000	.58	
Total (including beginning inventory) at retail		180,800			215,800		
Sales		(140,000)			(162,800)		
3. Ending Inventory at Retail		$ 40,800			$ 53,000		
4. Computation of ending inventory at Lifo cost:							
Ending inventory at retail deflated to base year retail prices:							
19B: $40,800 ÷ 1.02 . . .		$ 40,000					
19C: $53,000 ÷ 1.06 . . .					$ 50,000		
Base layer:							
At base year costs	$17,400			$ 17,400			
At base year retail prices . .		(30,000)			(30,000)		
Incremental layers from prior years: 19B				6,120	(10,000)		
Excess, new increments (or liquidation) at base year prices[a]		$ 10,000			$ 10,000		
Increment (or liquidation) at current year *retail* prices:							
19B: $10,000 × 1.02 . . .		$ 10,200					
19C: $10,000 × 1.06 . . .					$ 10,600		
Increment (or liquidation) at current year *costs*:							
19B: $10,200 × .60 . . .	6,120						
19C: $10,600 × .58 . . .				6,148			
Ending Inventory at Lifo Cost	$23,520			$ 29,668			

[a] When this difference is positive, there is a new incremental layer; when it is negative, there has been a partial liquidation of one or more prior layers. Such liquidations should be taken from the most recently added (i.e., the "last-in") layers.

Answer frame 1¹⁰

1. False. Cost is estimated to be $10,000. Computations:

Beginning inventory	$25,000
Purchases	15,000
Goods available, at cost	40,000
Less: Cost of goods sold*	(30,000)
Ending inventory (at cost) destroyed . .	$10,000

> * Markup on cost is 50%. Therefore,
> Sales = Cost of goods sold × 1.50
> $45,000 = Cost of goods sold × 1.50
> $45,000 ÷ 1.50 = Cost of goods sold
> $30,000 = Cost of goods sold

2. False. The gross profit method and the retail method are both methods of estimating inventories. The methods are used principally for *interim* (versus *annual*) reporting purposes. They are also used by auditors but only to estimate inventories as an adjunct to their more detailed audit tests of inventory balances.
3. False. Fifo unit cost (under any method) exceeds average unit cost only when costs are rising. When unit costs are falling, average cost exceeds Fifo cost. Furthermore, when there are no markdowns, cost and LCM, per the retail method, are the same.
4. True. The different forms of the retail method produce different inventory valuations due solely to computation of different cost ratios. In each case given in the text, the ending inventory at retail was $1,500—because the components of ending inventory at *retail* were the same.

If you missed any of the above, reread Frame 1¹⁰ before beginning Frame 2¹⁰, page 80.

Frame 2¹⁰ continued
Inventories and Income under Long-Term Construction Contracts

A special inventory problem arises with long-term construction contracts that extend beyond the end of the fiscal (accounting) period. In situations where financial statements are to be prepared prior to the end of the construction contract, there are two related problems: (*a*) valuation of the inventory of work in process and (*b*) the income (or loss) to be recognized on the income statement. There are two acceptable methods of accounting for long-term construction contracts:

1. The completed-contract method.
2. The percentage-of-completion method.

Completed-Contract Method.   This method, prior to completion of the contract, (*a*) reports no interim profit but rather recognizes all income on the contractual activities at the completion of the contract and (*b*) reports as construction in process inventory all costs incurred prior to completion of the contract, reduced by billings under the contract.

Percentage-of-Completion Method.   This method recognizes construction income (or loss) each year during the duration of the contract. This procedure requires a computation of the estimated income (or loss) each period and an estimate of the construction in process inventory. The estimated income is computed as a proportionate part of the total income expected on the contract; the proportionate part, each period, is based on the costs incurred to date related to the total costs expected at completion of the contract.

To illustrate the accounting for income (or loss) on long-term construction contracts under the completed-contract and percentage-of-completion methods, assume the following data:

1. Contract to construct a building for a flat fee of $1,500,000 starting January 1, 19A; estimated time to complete, 1½ years.
2. Progress billings to be made at the end of each month. Billings to be based on estimates of completion developed by the architects as of the 15th of each month.
3. Data covering the construction period:

	Cumulative	
	19A	19B
Costs incurred to date	$750,000	$1,350,000
Estimated costs to complete . . .	550,000	—
Progress billings to date	700,000	1,500,000
Progress collections to date . . .	670,000	1,500,000

The accounting entries for the duration of the contract under the completed-contract and the percentage-of-completion methods are given in parallel columns below:

	Completed Contract		Percentage of Completion	
19A				
1. Costs of construction:				
Construction in Process . . .	750,000		750,000	
Cash (or payables) . . .		750,000		750,000
2. Progress billings:				
Accounts receivable	700,000		700,000	
Billings on contracts . .		700,000		700,000
3. Cash collections:				
Cash	670,000		670,000	
Accounts receivable . . .		670,000		670,000
4. Recognition of income:				
Construction in process . . .			115,385*	
Construction income . .				115,385

* Computations:

$$\frac{\text{Total cumulative costs}}{\text{Total estimated costs}} \times \text{Estimated total income} - \text{Income already recognized} = \text{Current} - \text{period income.}$$

$$\frac{\$750,000}{\$750,000 + \$550,000} \times [\$1,500,000 - (\$750,000 + \$550,000)] - \$0 = \underline{\underline{\$115,385}}$$

	Completed Contract		Percentage of Completion	
19B				
1. Costs of construction:				
Construction in process . . .	600,000		600,000	
Cash (or payables) . . .		600,000		600,000
2. Progress billings:				
Accounts receivable	800,000		800,000	
Billings on contracts . .		800,000		800,000
3. Cash collections:				
Cash . . . . : . .	830,000		830,000	
Accounts receivable . .		830,000		830,000
4. Recognition of income:				
Billings on contracts	1,500,000		1,500,000	
Construction in process .		1,350,000	1,465,385*	
Construction income . .		150,000		34,615†

* $1,465,385 = $750,000 + $600,000 + $115,385.

† Computations:

$$\frac{\$1,350,000}{\$1,350,000} \times (\$1,500,000 - \$1,350,000) - \$115,385 = \$34,615, \text{ or}$$

$$\$1,500,000 - \$1,350,000 - \$115,385 = \$34,615.$$

At the end of 19A, the financial statements of this company will report (in summarized form):

	Completed Contract	Percentage of Completion
Balance Sheet		
Current Assets:		
Accounts receivable ($700,000 − $670,000)	$30,000	$ 30,000
Inventories:		
Construction in process	$750,000	$865,385
Less: Billings on contracts	700,000	700,000
Equity in inventory	50,000	165,385
Income Statement		
Construction income	$ –0–	$115,385

The percentage-of-completion method generally results in a better matching of periodic revenue and expense. But percentage of completion should be used only when estimates of (a) cost to complete, (b) progress toward completion, and (c) total profit can be determined with reasonable accuracy, and (d) ultimate realization of the contractual amount is reasonably assured. In other cases the completed-contract method should be utilized. Either method is acceptable for federal income tax purposes.

Reporting Inventories on the Balance Sheet

Inventories normally are reported on the balance sheet at cost (in accordance with the cost principle) as current assets. Certain exceptions to cost, such as lower of cost or market and realizable value, are permitted under specified conditions. The accounting principle of adequate disclosure requires that the valuation method (cost, lower of cost or market, etc.) and the inventory flow method (Fifo, Lifo, etc.) be clearly indicated on the balance sheet. Also, any change in the methods of handling inventories, and the dollar effect of such changes, should be reported. Merchandise "on consignment" must be reported as inventory on the balance sheet of the consignor (but not the consignee) since the consignor retains legal title until the goods are actually sold by the consignee. Any unusual aspects of inventory must also be reported.

Determine whether each of the following two statements is true or false.

_____ 1. The retail-Lifo method of estimating inventory cost utilizes aspects of both (a) dollar-value Lifo (through use of price indexes) and (b) the retail estimation method (through use of the cost-retail ratio).

_____ 2. Prior to completion of a long-term construction contract, the percentage-of-completion method will normally report a larger balance in the Construction in Process account than the completed-contract method will report.

Now work the following problems that utilize the text material of Frame 2¹⁰.

3. Refer to Illustration 10–1 on the retail-Lifo inventory method. Assume that the ending inventory, at retail, for 19C had been $37,100 (instead of $53,000). Hold all other factors constant and compute the ending inventory for 19C at estimated Lifo cost, using the retail method.

4. Refer to the data and entries given on page 83 to illustrate the accounting for inventories and income under long-term construction contracts. Present the data that would be reported in the 19B financial statements.

Now refer to Answer Frame 2¹⁰, page 86.

chapter 11

LIABILITIES AND INCOME TAXES

Frame 1[11]

Nature of Liabilities

Liabilities are debts or obligations to pay others. In accounting, liabilities are classified as either current or long term. This distinction has meaning in financial analysis with respect to assessing the current (or long-term) financial position of the enterprise. This chapter deals mostly with current liabilities, and Chapter 19 covers long-term bond liabilities.

The two basic problems in accounting for liabilities are (a) identification and (b) valuation. Unlike *assets* (most of which are tangible), all liabilities are *intangible* because they represent the creditors' equity (claims) in the assets of the business. Therefore, it is easy to understate liabilities (as reported on the balance sheet) by outright omission of a particular liability (e.g., omission of a year-end salary expense accrual).

Valuation of liabilities and valuation of assets are essentially synonymous because liabilities are generally incurred to acquire assets, even though the asset may have already been used up (as an expense). And the cost of the asset purchased with a liability is literally the *present value* of the liability. This means, in effect, that liabilities should be valued at the present value of the future payments necessary to eliminate the debt. To illustrate this application of present value concepts, assume that a company acquired a machine for which it promised to pay $10,000 at the end of three years. The cost of the machine is not $10,000; it is the *present value* of $10,000. And this principle is equally applicable to current obligations (of one, two, or three months). However, the *amount* of the difference between the present value and the maturity value of current liabilities is less than the difference for a similar but long-term liability. And because this difference (between present value and maturity value) is usually quite small (i.e., immaterial) for current liabilities, it is sometimes ignored, in which case current liabilities are reported on the balance sheet at *maturity value*. For an application that illustrates present value accounting for the cost of inventory and the related *accounts payable,* see Frame 2[8].

Another aspect of the problem of valuing liabilities concerns the fact that some liabilities are known to exist, but the specific amount is not known with certainty. In such a case the amount of the liability should be estimated, and the liability will be reported as an estimated liability. An example of an estimated liability is a warranty obligation for goods sold with a guarantee.

Current Liabilities

Current liabilities are those obligations (known or estimated as to amount) the liquidation of which is reasonably expected to require the use of funds classified as current assets or through the creation of other current liabilities. The principal types of current liabilities are (a) accounts payable (trade), (b) special accounts payable, (c) short-term notes payable, (c) cash dividends payable, (d) funds held as returnable

Answer frame 2¹⁰

1. True. This explains why retail Lifo is frequently referred to as dollar-value retail Lifo.
2. True. The amount of the difference will be the amount of estimated construction income which, under percentage of completion, is debited to Construction in Process as costs are incurred under the contract. Under completed contract, no income is recognized until the contract activities are completed; hence the Construction in Process account is reported under completed contract at the amount of costs incurred *only*.
3. $20,460.

		Cost	Retail
Computations:			
Cost ratio for 19C, as given in illustration 10–1	.58		
Ending inventory, at retail, as given in the problem . . .			$37,100
Price index to deflate to base year			÷ 1.06
Ending inventory, at retail, stated in base year dollars . .			$35,000
Comprised of:		Cost	Retail
Base layer, as given in Illustration 10–1		$17,400	$30,000
Remaining portion of 19B layer, at base year retail prices			5,000
Price index to restate to 19B dollars			× 1.02
19B layer, stated in 19B dollars at retail			5,100
Cost ratio to convert retail to cost			× .60
19B layer, at 19B cost		3,060	
Ending Inventory at Lifo cost		$20,460	

4. Balance Sheet 19B:
    Nothing reported because (*a*) all receivables were collected and (*b*) all inventory was transferred to buyer.
    Income Statement 19B:

	Completed Contract	Percentage of Completion
Construction Income . . .	150,000	$34,615

If you missed any of the above questions, you should reread Frame 2¹⁰ before proceeding. Then you should take Sample Examination 2 that covers Chapters 7–10, beginning on page 130. Then continue reading with Chapter 11.

Frame 1¹¹ continued

deposits, (*e*) funds collected for third parties, (*f*) accrued liabilities, (*g*) deferred revenues, (*h*) estimated short-term liabilities, and (*i*) current installments on long-term debts. Accounts and notes payable are the most common current liabilities; they should be reported separately. Notes payable secured by collateral (pledged or mortgaged assets) should be indicated by footnote or as follows:

Investments:		Current Liabilities:	
Stock in X Corp., at cost (pledged for		Notes payable (secured by stock in	
$1,000 note payable to Bank Y) $5,000		X Corp.). $1,000	

It is common for government taxing authorities to require businesses to collect taxes from their employees and customers for remittance to the governmental agencies. These collections give rise to current liabilities. To illustrate, assume there is a 4% sales tax and that sales for the period were $100,000; the entry to record the sales and the related liability would be:

Cash or accounts receivable	104,000	
Sales		100,000
Sales taxes payable		4,000

To remit the taxes:

Sales taxes payable	4,000	
Cash		4,000

Accrued Liabilities

Accrued liabilities arise through accounting recognition (normally via adjusting entries) of expenses which have been incurred but have not been paid at the end of the accounting period. For example, assume the last payroll of the year was paid on December 24 and that wages unpaid for the last six days amounted to $8,000. The following adjusting entry to record the accrued liability would be made (disregarding payroll taxes):

Wage expense	8,000	
Wages payable		8,000

Deferred Credits

Deferred credits, as a balance sheet caption, are sometimes erroneously positioned after liabilities and above owners' equity on some companies' balance sheets. One variously finds under this caption *four* different types of items:

a. Deferred revenues, such as the unearned subscription revenue of a publisher.
b. Certain credits arising from internal transactions, such as deferred repairs (an accrued repair liability).
c. Credits arising from income tax allocation procedures (to be covered in Frame 3[11] of this chapter).
d. Miscellaneous credits, such as premium on bonds payable.

In summary, all items included in the above four captions *are* liabilities. This follows from the fact that they are *not* elements of owners' equity. Therefore, based on the financial position model (Assets = Liabilities + Owners' Equity), the credit balance items are liabilities if they are not elements of owners' equity or contra assets. Consequently, deferred credits should be reported as either current or long-term liabilities, depending on whether or not they make a claim against current assets.

Tax and Bonus Considerations

It is not unusual to encounter employment contracts that provide for a *bonus* to be paid to the officers of a company under specified conditions that usually are related to some derivative of net income. The bonus may be computed in a number of different ways; the bonus contract will specify the method. A bonus should be treated as an operating expense and should be set up as a current liability pending payment.

True or false?

_____ 1. Liabilities should, in general, be recorded in the accounts and reported in the financial statements at *present value*.

_____ 2. Accrued liabilities are uncertain as to existence, but the amount can be reasonably estimated; therefore, accrued liabilities are accorded formal treatment in the accounts as though they were *real* liabilities.

_____ 3. Recording assets that are acquired with debt, at the present value of the obligation, understates asset values.

_____ 4. Deferred credits should be reported on the balance sheet beneath liabilities and above owners' equity.

Now refer to Answer Frame 1[11], page 88.

Answer frame 1¹¹

1. True. This important concept is sometimes not applied to current liabilities due to the perceived immateriality of the difference between the present value and the (higher) maturity value of the obligation.

2. False. Accrued liabilities are *real* liabilities. They are certain as to existence, *and* the amount is either known with certainty or it can be reasonably estimated. Finally, due to these factors, accrued liabilities are given formal accounting treatment.

    In a sense, the title "accrued" liabilities is a misnomer because all liabilities are *accrued*. This points to the common usage of the term "accrued liabilities," which by convention refers to liabilities for which no formal document (such as an invoice) is received as a request for payment.

3. False. Recording assets that are acquired with debt, at the maturity value of the obligation, *overstates* the cost of the asset (by the amount of interest included in the maturity value). Therefore, assets that are acquired with debt should be recorded at the present value of the debt. For examples, see Frame 2 of Chapter 8 and Frame 1 of Chapter 12.

4. False. To so report deferred credits suggests that they are neither liabilities *nor* owners' equity. The accounting model has no category to accommodate such a classification. Deferred credits *are* liabilities.

If you missed any of the above, reread Frame 1¹¹ before beginning Frame 2¹¹ below.

Frame 2¹¹

Estimated Liabilities

Known liabilities the amounts of which are uncertain at the balance sheet date, should be accorded formal accounting treatment in the accounts. The amount of the liability should be realistically estimated on the basis of all information available. The account title should clearly indicate that the amount is an estimate; for example, appropriate titles are Estimated Property Taxes Payable, Estimated Warranty Liability, and Estimated Premium Claims Outstanding.

To illustrate the accounting for an estimated liability, assume that Johnson Company sells $30,000 of its products in 19D subject to a two-year warranty as to materials and workmanship. Based on Johnson's past experience, it appears that 2% of all its sales are returned for repairs due to defects. During 19D, Johnson actually paid $500 for warranty claims. The accounting entries for 19D could be summarized as follows:

To record 19D warranty expense and 19D addition to estimated liability:

Warranty expense (an operating expense)	600	
Estimated warranty liability (.02 × $30,000)		600

To pay cash against the estimated liability:

Estimated warranty liability	500	
Cash		500

Also assume that, *prior to* making the above two entries, Johnson had a credit balance of $250 in the Estimated Warranty Liability account. After making the 19D entries above, Johnson's estimated warranty liability, as recorded in the accounts, is $350 ($250 + $600 − $500).

The major point of this illustration is that the *matching* principle requires that the *total* expense of a period be matched against the revenue of the period, regardless of *when* the cash outlays associated with the expense are incurred.

Contingent Liabilities

Contingent liabilities are *potential* rather than *real* liabilities. That is, they have not become bona fide obligations *yet* because any legal indebtedness of the entity depends on some future event or circumstance.

FASB *Statement No. 5* identifies three basic types of contingencies:

1. Contingent losses (liabilities) that should be recorded in the accounts as though they already had materialized.
2. Contingent losses (liabilities) that should *not* be recorded as real liabilities, but which should nevertheless be disclosed in the financial statements.
3. Contingent assets (gains).

In general, contingent gains are *not recorded, nor* are they *reported,* due to the influence of conservatism on accounting practice.

FASB *Statement No. 5* provides two criteria for distinguishing between the two categories of contingent losses. Both of the following criteria must be met for a contingent loss to be recorded as a loss and reported as such in the income statement:

1. It is *probable* that an asset has been impaired or that a liability has been incurred as a result of the factors underlying the contingency.
2. The amount of the loss can be reasonably estimated.

Examples of contingent losses (and related contingent liabilities) that do *not* meet the two criteria are:

1. Lawsuits pending.
2. Notes receivable discounted. When a note receivable is discounted at a bank (i.e., endorsed and sold to the bank), the endorser remains contingently liable to the bank for payment of the note until the maturity date of the note, when the contingency expires.
3. Accommodation endorsement (i.e., cosignature of a note payable along with the maker of the note).

It is clear that the dollar amount of each of these types of contingent losses (liabilities) cannot normally be estimated with precision. Therefore such *contingencies* are not recorded as losses. Nevertheless, they must be reported as *contingent* losses in the financial statements to accord with the accounting principle of adequate disclosure. Three principal methods are used to disclose these types of contingent losses:

1. Notes to the financial statements.
2. Parenthetical note.
3. Appropriation of retained earnings.

Examples of contingent losses that *do* meet the two criteria are:

1. Bad debt losses on receivables.
2. Warranty expenses.
3. Expenses associated with offers of premiums (prizes) as an inducement for customers to buy the seller's products.

At this point the reader should note that (*a*) bad debt losses are accrued (as covered in Chapter 7) and (*b*) *estimated expenses* (and liabilities) such as those that arise from warranties and premium offers are accounted for in the manner covered in the first part ("Estimated Liabilities") of this frame.

Determine whether each of the following statements is true or false.

———— 1. Contingencies of all types (gains and losses) should not be recorded prior to the time when they materialize due to the accounting principle of conservatism.

———— 2. Whether a contingency is recorded in the accounts (versus being merely reported in a footnote, e.g.) depends solely on whether the amount of the contingency can be reasonably estimated.

———— 3. The contingent loss associated with a lawsuit should never be recorded as a loss prior to the decision of the court.

———— 4. The expense associated with an estimated liability should be accounted for on the accrual basis (as opposed to the cash basis) in accordance with the matching principle of accounting.

Now compare your responses with those given in Answer Frame 2[11], page 92.

Frame 3[11]

Accounting for Income Taxes—Timing Differences

Income taxes are regarded as one of the expenses of doing business. As a result they are accounted for on the accrual basis like all other expenses. In the simplest form, the income tax entry for a corporation is:[1]

Income tax expense XXXX
    Income tax payable   XXXX

In this highly simplified example, the dollar amounts of the debit to expense and the credit to the liability are the same. In actual practice, however, this equality often will not occur. Common types of items that cause differences between the debit to income tax expense and the credit to income tax payable are:

1. Differences in the *timing* of the recognition of revenue or expense for tax and financial reporting ("book") purposes. These are referred to as *timing differences,* and there are five categories of timing differences:

    a. Revenues or gains which are included in taxable income one or more periods *after* they are included in pretax accounting income; for example, gross profit on installment sales.

    b. Expenses or losses which are deducted in determining taxable income one or more periods *after* they are deducted in determining pretax accounting income; for example, estimated (accrued) warranty costs.

    c. Revenues or gains which are included in taxable income *before* they are included in pretax accounting income; for example, rent revenue collected in advance.

    d. Expenses or losses which are deducted in determining taxable income *before* they are deducted in determining pretax accounting income; for example, depreciation on an accelerated basis for tax purposes, but on a straight-line basis for book purposes.

    e. Accounting for the investment tax credit on a deferral basis for book purposes and on a flow-through basis for tax purposes (covered in Frame 1 of Chapter 12).

2. Prior period adjustments to Retained Earnings, where the prior period adjustment is being made for

---

[1] Throughout this discussion, it is assumed that the corporation makes one entry, at the end of the year, to record its total income tax for the year. The assumption is not realistic, for corporations are required to make quarterly payments for income taxes. Then the year-end entry records the balance of income tax expense and payable that have not been previously recorded. Mastery of the text material will enable the student to master the concepts involved in accounting for income taxes, the unrealistic assumption notwithstanding.

an item that had the effect of over- or understating income before tax and also income tax expense for a specific prior period.
3. Tax loss carryforwards (to be covered in the final section of Frame 4[11]).

Permanent Differences

In addition to the above three categories of timing differences, there is another category of "differences" in income tax accounting. This category is known as *permanent differences;* permanent differences involve basic differences in the *definitions* of specific revenues and expenses for tax and financial reporting purposes. In the context of income tax accounting, the *tax* definition of the item is relevant; in this context the financial accounting definition is totally irrelevant. Therefore, the tax definition of the item is used for purposes of computing *both* income tax expense and income tax payable. Consequently, for an item that constitutes a *permanent difference,* there is *no* difference between income tax expense and income tax payable. Examples of permanent differences are:

a. Tax-exempt interest revenue earned on investments in municipal bonds. This interest revenue is never taxed.
b. *Statutory depletion* on natural resources. The tax regulations allow businesses that extract and sell natural resources to deduct from taxable income a stipulated percentage of gross revenue as depletion. In many cases the total statutory depletion over time exceeds the total cost of the asset being depleted. The income tax on the difference between statutory depletion and cost depletion *never* has to be paid.
c. Goodwill. Amortization expense for goodwill is *never* a tax-deductible expense.

To illustrate the accounting for income taxes, assume in the following examples that Corporation STU had the following data for the year 19C:

Net income before income taxes	$35,000
1. Accelerated depreciation for tax purposes	12,000
Straight-line depreciation for book purposes (included as a deduction in arriving at net income before taxes above)	10,000
2. Prior period adjustment—operating income *before* taxes in 19B overstated due to accounting error in 19B, discovered in 19C (not included in net income before taxes above because prior period adjustments affect Retained Earnings directly, not the period's net income)	1,500
3. Tax-free interest revenue earned (included as revenue in arriving at net income before taxes above)	1,000
Income tax rate	40%

The entries that follow will consider each of the three items *individually*—in conjunction with net income before taxes of $35,000. First, let us illustrate the general form of the 19C income tax entry, prior to giving effect to items 1–3 listed above. The basic (unmodified) entry is:

Income tax expense (.40 × $35,000) 14,000
   Income tax payable 14,000

If we introduce item 1 (the depreciation differential) along with net income before taxes, the entry is:

Income tax expense (.40 × $35,000) 14,000
   Income tax payable [.40 × ($35,000 + $10,000 − $12,000)] . . . 13,200
   Deferred income taxes [.40 × ($12,000 − $10,000)] 800

Answer frame 2¹¹

1. False. Contingent *losses* that (*a*) have *probably* already occurred and (*b*) can be reasonably estimated as to amount should be recorded as losses. The statement would be true if "losses" were not included therein.

2. False. Whether a contingency is recorded depends on (*a*) whether it involves a contingent gain or a contingent loss, (*b*) whether the *loss* has probably already occurred, and (*c*) whether the amount of the loss can be reasonably estimated.

3. False. If the defendant is confident that the court will render an adverse verdict and if the amount of the loss can be reasonably estimated, the defendant should record a loss and report it in the income statement even though the lawsuit is still pending. This company will also record a *real* liability and report it in the balance sheet.

   The student can generally resolve accounting issues of this nature by asking this question: Would knowledge of the item in question (pending lawsuit in this case) affect my decision to buy (or hold or sell) the stock of the defendant company? If the answer to this crucial question is "Yes," then the item *may* need to be disclosed. If the answer is "No," then the item *may not* need to be disclosed. In potentially controversial disclosure issues such as this one, it is advisable for the practicing accountant to consult with other accountants as well as with legal counsel prior to making the final decision as to whether or not to disclose the item in question.

4. True. This statement represents sound business and accounting reasoning.

If you missed any of the above, reread Frame 2¹¹ before beginning Frame 3¹¹, page 90.

Frame 3¹¹ continued

This entry exemplifies *interperiod* tax allocation, that is, the allocation of the income tax expense of $14,000 to 19C even though the income tax (currently) payable is only $13,200. In a sense income tax allocation represents accrual accounting (versus cash accounting) for income taxes. The reader should note that the straight-line depreciation will exceed the accelerated depreciation in the later years of use of the fixed assets. In those later years, the income tax payable will be greater than the income tax expense, and the Deferred Income Taxes account will then be debited. In fact, this illustrates the nature of a timing difference (versus a permanent difference). Timing differences *reverse* over time; permanent differences do not reverse because they are permanent.

If item 1 represents the only complicating factor, Corporation STU will report net income of $21,000 ($35,000 − $14,000) on its income statement for 19C. On its 19C year-end balance sheet STU will report $13,200 of income tax payable under current liabilities and $800 of deferred income taxes under either current liabilities or long-term liabilities, depending on the anticipated time when the company expects to have to pay the $800. If a *different* item of timing difference had given rise to a *debit* balance in deferred taxes, then STU would have had a Deferred Income Tax (expense), and the *debit* balance of $800 would have been reported as either a current asset or a deferred charge, depending on the anticipated time when the company expects to use the prepayment to reduce a future income tax payable.

Next, we introduce item 2 (the prior period adjustment) along with net income before taxes. We assume that the tax effect of the prior period adjustment is being used to reduce the current income tax liability—rather than being used to obtain a cash refund from the Internal Revenue Service. The income tax entry is:

Income tax expense (.40 × $35,000)	14,000	
Income tax payable [.40 × ($35,000 − $1,500)]		13,400
Prior period adjustment to retained earnings—tax		
effect of accounting error in 19B (.40 × $1,500)		600

It is worth noting that the prior period adjustment had *no* effect on 19C reported net income. This of course is consistent with the definition of a prior period adjustment, which bypasses the income statement entirely and directly adjusts the Retained Earnings account. Therefore, the 19C income statement will report net income of $21,000 ($35,000 − $14,000).

Next, we introduce item 3 (the tax-free interest revenue) along with net income before taxes. The income entry for 19C is:

Income tax expense [.40 × ($35,000 − $1,000)] 13,600
    Income tax payable [.40 × $35,000 − $1,000)]   13,600

Note that this item of *permanent difference* (the Internal Revenue Code does not define interest revenue earned on certain securities as income for tax purposes; however, for financial accounting purposes, tax-free interest revenue is every bit as much a revenue as Sales Revenue or Gain on Sale of Land) gives rise to no difference between income tax expense and income tax payable. Contrast this treatment with the treatment accorded the *timing difference* on depreciation illustrated above.

Finally, we combine net income before tax of $35,000 and *all* three complicating factors into Corporation STU's *single* income tax entry for 19C. First, it is usually helpful to prepare a schedule that summarizes all the relevant items entering into a determination of income tax expense and income tax payable.

Income Tax Expense to Be Matched against Revenue on the Income Statement		Income Tax Payable (the current payable to the Internal Revenue Service—a current liability on the balance sheet)
$35,000	Net income before tax . . .	$35,000
	Add back straight-line depreciation	10,000
	Deduct accelerated depreciation	(12,000)
	Deduct prior period adjustment	(1,500)
(1,000)	Deduct tax-free interest revenue	(1,000)
34,000		30,500
× .4	Tax rate	× .4
$13,600		$12,200

Thus, Corporation STU's 19C income tax entry is:

Income tax expense (from the schedule) 13,600
    Income tax payable (from the schedule)   12,200
    Prior period adjustment—tax effect of accounting error in 19B . . .   600
    Deferred income taxes (due to the depreciation differential) . . .   800

Based on the above data, Corporation STU's 19C financial statements will report the following relative to its income taxes. Assume that 19B ending (19C beginning) Retained Earnings balance was $65,000.

Income Statement 19C:

Net income before income taxes	$35,000
Income tax expense	13,600
Net income	$21,400

Statement of Retained Earnings 19C:

Balance, beginning of year 19C, as previously reported		$65,000
Deduct prior period adjustment (see Note 2):		
19B operating income overstated	($1,500)	
Less: Income tax effect	600	(900)
Balance, beginning of 19C, as adjusted		64,100
Add net income for 19C		21,400
Balance, End of 19C		$85,500

Note 2.   Prior period adjustment. During 19C, the Corporation made an accounting error that had the effect of overstating 19B net income by $900 (net of income tax). Accordingly, the correction is recorded as a Prior Period Adjustment to Retained Earnings. This adjustment has no effect on net income for 19C.

Balance Sheet 19C:

Current Liabilities:

Income tax payable	$12,200

Long-Term liabilities:

Deferred income taxes (assumed to be *long term* because it is anticipated that it will take several years for straight-line depreciation to exceed accelerated depreciation)	800

Intraperiod Income Tax Allocation

It was stated above that *timing* differences in the recognition of revenue or expense for tax and book purposes give rise to the need for *interperiod* income tax allocation. There is another type of income tax allocation known as *intraperiod* tax allocation. Most intermediate accounting students are already familiar with intraperiod tax allocation because it merely involves *reporting* the income tax associated with a particular type of income along with that income—wherever the income is reported in the financial statements. For example, using the above data, Corporation STU reported $13,600 of income tax expense on its income statement and a *net* prior period adjustment of $900 ($1,500 less tax effect of $600) on its statement of retained earnings. *Another* example of an item that causes a need for intraperiod tax allocation is an extraordinary gain (or loss) that has an income tax effect.

True or false?

_____ 1.   If a corporation earned one revenue, namely $1,000 of *tax-free* interest, during a year, its income tax expense and payable for the year would be zero. Its net income for the year would be $1,000.

_____ 2.   The *only* items that give rise to the need for interperiod income tax allocation are timing differences.

_____ 3.   Intraperiod tax allocation is a substitute for interperiod tax allocation.

_____ 4.   Deferred income tax credits are always classified as *long-term* liabilities, and deferred income tax debits are always classified as deferred charges (i.e., *long-term* prepaid expenses).

Now refer to Answer Frame 3[11], page 96.

Frame 4[11]

Accounting for Income Taxes (continued)[2]—Tax Loss Carrybacks

If a company incurs an operating loss during a year that follows a year or years when the company paid income taxes, it can generally receive a refund from the Internal Revenue Service to the extent that the current loss is offset by prior years' incomes. For example, assume that Jones Company's earnings for the years 19A–19D are as follows:

	19A	19B	19C	19D
Net income (loss) before income tax . .	$25,000	$18,000	$14,000	($46,000)

If the income tax rate is 40% in all years, Jones Company can file its 19D income tax return and thereupon receive a refund of $18,400 (.40 × $46,000) because the loss is totally absorbed by earnings in 19A–19C. The tax law provides that losses may be:

a. Carried *back* three years, to the third previous year *first, then* to the second previous year, and *then* the previous year, and if not absorbed in the carryback.
b. Carried *forward* five years, beginning with the first year after the loss year and continuing with the second year, and so forth, *in order.*

Jones' 19D entry to record its income tax saving for the year would be:

Receivable from IRS for tax loss carryback (.40 × $46,000) 18,400
Income tax refund (or income tax expense)   18,400

Jones Company's income statement will report a *net* loss of $27,600 ($46,000 − $18,400) for 19D.

If the tax rate had been 35% in 19A–19C and was 40% in 19D, the refund would have been $16,100 (.35 × $46,000), in which case Jones Company would have reported a 19D net loss of $29,900 ($46,000 − $16,100). This illustrates an important point with respect to tax loss carrybacks *and* carryforwards: carry back and forward losses, *not* taxes on losses. That is, carry back the loss to the year when taxable income was earned and apply the tax rate that existed in the carryback year to the computation of the refund. Do not apply the tax rate in the loss year—unless of course the same tax rate applies to both years. This same principle applies to tax loss carryforwards as well.

Tax Loss Carryforwards

In the example above Jones Company's 19D loss was more than offset by 19A–19C operating profits. Thus, there was no loss carryforward. The accounting for tax loss carryforwards is slightly more complex than the accounting for carrybacks because of the uncertainty that the company will *ever* earn future taxable income sufficient to realize the benefit associated with a tax loss *carryforward.*

This uncertainty presents an interesting proposition. If the company does *later* earn sufficient income, then *ex post* the company *should have* recorded in the loss year an asset for the tax loss carryforward. The problem is that at the time the loss is incurred, there is no way to know with certainty that the loss will be absorbed by future earnings. This problem is similar to many other accounting problems that are resolved by appealing to a standard convention promulgated by the APB or the FASB. In this case, *APB Opinion No. 11* states that the effects of tax loss carryforwards ordinarily should *not* be recorded prior to the time when they are realized (i.e., when *later* income is earned). However, in a few limited cases, it is permissible to reduce the pretax operating loss (in the loss year) by any *projected* tax saving on the loss.

---

[2] In order to keep the following discussion (Frame 4[11]) manageable, we assume in the remainder of this chapter that there are *no timing differences, no permanent differences, nor prior period adjustments.* Thus in the examples that follow, the income tax expense and income tax payable for each year are equivalent except for any difference that is caused by a tax loss carryforward.

Answer frame 3¹¹

1. True. Tax-free interest is an item that constitutes a permanent difference—in the definitions of revenue used by taxing authorities and financial accounting theory. The IRS does *not* define certain interest revenue as *revenue*—for *tax purposes*. Therefore, it is deducted from net income before income tax in computing income taxes *payable*. And because tax-free interest is an item of permanent difference, it is also deducted from net income before tax in computing income tax expense.

2. True. Interperiod income tax allocation is manifested by a balance (either debit or credit) in the Deferred Income Tax account. The only items that can underlie the need to debit or credit the Deferred Income Tax account are items of revenue or expense that are recognized for book purposes in one period and for tax purposes in a different period (i.e., timing differences).

3. False. The two types of income tax allocation are entirely different and serve different purposes altogether. *Interperiod* income tax allocation involves matching against the revenue of a period the related income tax expense for the period regardless of *when* those taxes will be paid. *Intraperiod* income tax allocation, on the other hand, simply involves *reporting* directly beneath each major source of income (in one period's financial statements) the income tax that is related to that source. For example, if a company had $20,000 of net income before tax and before extraordinary items (and this income was taxed at 40%) and $5,000 of an extraordinary gain (taxed at 25%), the lower part of its income statement would appear as follows:

Net income before income tax and extraordinary items		$20,000
Less: Income tax expense (.40 × $20,000) . . .		8,000
Net income before extraordinary items		12,000
Extraordinary gain—source stated	$5,000	
Less: Income tax expense on the gain (.25 × $5,000)	1,250	3,750
Net Income		$15,750

The separation of total income tax expense of $9,250 into its separate elements ($8,000 and $1,250) evidences *intraperiod* tax allocation. No evidence of *interperiod* tax allocation is given in this illustration because we do not know whether any timing differences exist. But the two types of tax allocation are *not* substitutes.

4. False. Whether deferred tax credits (or debits) are *long term* or *current* depends entirely on the time span over which the credits (or debits) are expected to exist. This, in turn, depends on the nature of the item that underlies the deferral of tax. In the illustration used in the text (accelerated depreciation for tax purposes and straight-line for book purposes), the deferred tax credit was classified as long term on the assumption that this occurred in the early years of use of a fixed asset. In this case, it would be several years before straight-line (book) depreciation would exceed accelerated (tax) depreciation; as a result, the deferred tax credit would remain on STU's books for several years, and this implies that the deferred tax credit should be classified as long term.

   If the text illustration had occurred in the middle years of use of the fixed asset (e.g., the third year of a seven-year asset), a portion of the deferred tax credit would have been classified as a current liability.

   If a deferred tax *credit* arises because a company records revenue on installment sales (*a*) on the sales basis for *book* purposes and (*b*) on the collection basis for *tax* purposes, then at least some of the tax credit will be classified as current—as long as the company expects *some* collections in the next period.

If you missed any of the above, reread Frame 3¹¹ before beginning Frame 4¹¹, page 95.

Frame 4[11] continued

This is permitted only when it is *virtually* certain that the tax benefit will be earned via future incomes. An example of such a case is an operating loss that resulted from a single, isolated event.

To illustrate the accounting for tax loss carryforwards, let us now assume that the income tax rate is 40% in all years and that Jones Company's earnings for 19A–19D are as follows:

	19A	19B	19C	19D
Net income (loss) before income tax .	$5,000	$18,000	$14,000	($46,000)
		$37,000		

At this point Jones must decide whether it expects *beyond any reasonable doubt* to earn $9,000 of taxable income in the five years 19E–19I. Ordinarily, the answer to this question would be "No." Under these circumstances, Jones' entry to record its 19D income taxes would be:

Receivable from IRS on tax loss carryback (.40 × $37,000)	14,800	
Income tax refund (or income tax expense)		14,800

And for 19D, Jones would report a net loss of $31,200 ($46,000 − $14,800). Then if Jones Company earns $9,000 ($46,000 − $37,000) of taxable income in any one or combination of the years 19E–19I, the company will record an Extraordinary Gain for the tax saving. For example, assume that Jones Company earns $10,000 in 19E. Its 19E income tax entry will be:

Income tax expense (.40 × $10,000)	4,000	
Extraordinary gain—realization of previously unrecorded tax loss carryforward (.40 × $9,000)		3,600
Income tax payable [.40 × ($10,000 − $9,000)]		400

Use the same data, but now assume that Jones Company is virtually certain it will earn $9,000 during 19E–19I. Its 19D income tax entry:

Receivable from IRS on tax loss carry*back* (.40 × $37,000)	14,800	
Asset—benefit of tax loss carry*forward* [.40 × ($46,000 − $37,000)] . .	3,600	
Income tax refund (or income tax expense) (.40 × $46,000) . . .		18,400

Under these circumstances, Jones' 19D income statement will report a net loss of $27,600 ($46,000 − $18,400), and its 19D year-end balance sheet will report (in addition to the Receivable) the account entitled Asset—Benefit of Tax Loss Carryforward at $3,600 in the Other Asset category.

Then, in the years 19E–19I, Jones either *will* or *will not* earn the income sufficient to realize the benefit of the carryforward. If Jones does earn $9,000 of income, the asset will be credited in lieu of Income Tax Payable. If Jones fails to earn some or all of the $9,000, the asset will be credited and an Extraordinary Loss recognized—probably in year 19I—because it will probably take five years before it will be certain that the benefit will never be realized.

In conclusion, we return to a statement made near the beginning of Frame 3[11]. The statement was that tax loss carryforwards can cause differences between the debit to Income Tax Expense and the credit to Income Tax Payable *for a year* (see item number 3 in the first list presented in Frame 3[11]). The foregoing discussion should shed considerable light on that statement. Also, we should mention that the entire discussion of accounting for income taxes (Frames 3[11] and 4[11]) is based on the provisions of *APB Opinion No. 11.*

Now gauge your progress by answering true or false to the following questions.

_____ 1.   The *realization* of a tax loss carryforward is known with certainty, whereas realization of tax loss carrybacks is not known with certainty.

Questions 2–5 are independent, but they all use the following data:

Let Jones Company's earnings history and effective tax rates be:

	19A	19B	19C	19D	19E	19F	19G	19H	19I
Taxable income (loss)	$1,000	$2,000	$4,000	($8,000)	($3,000)	$3,000	$0	$10,000	$6,000
Tax rate	30%	30%	35%	◄——————40%——————►			◄——45%——►		

_____ 2.   Jones Company's total income tax payable for 19A–19C is $2,300.

_____ 3.   Jones Company's refund associated with its 19D loss is $3,200.

_____ 4.   Assume that in 19D Jones Company believes beyond any reasonable doubt that it will realize all the tax benefits associated with its 19D loss. Its 19D net loss will be reported at $4,800.

_____ 5.   If Jones Company recorded *no* tax loss carryforwards, Jones Company's entry to record its income taxes for 19H is:

Income tax expense	4,500	
Income tax payable		4,050
Extraordinary gain—realization of previously unrecorded tax loss carryforward from 19E . . .		450

You should now compare your answers with those given in Answer Frame 4[11], page 100.

chapter 12

OPERATIONAL ASSETS: PROPERTY, PLANT, AND EQUIPMENT—ACQUISITION, USE, AND RETIREMENT

Frame 1[12]

Nature of Operational Assets

Operational assets (property, plant, and equipment) are those properties and rights which a business retains more or less permanently, not for sale but for utilization in carrying out normal operations. Operational assets, also referred to as fixed assets, generally are classified as follows for business and accounting purposes:

1. Tangible (property, plant, and equipment)—those having a physical form. There are three subclasses:
    a. Those subject to depreciation, such as buildings and equipment.
    b. Those subject to depletion, such as mineral deposits, oil wells, and timber tracts.
    c. Those not subject to depreciation or depletion, such as land.
2. Intangibles—those having no physical form; their value depends solely upon rights which they confer upon their owner. Examples are patents, copyrights, franchises, and goodwill.

Intangible fixed assets are covered in Chapter 14. Idle plant facilities, land held as a prospective plant site, and obsolete, unused facilities should not be classified as operational assets but as "other" assets on the balance sheet.

Capital versus Revenue Expenditures

Capital expenditures relate to the acquisition of future benefits (assets) that extend over *more than one* accounting period; hence they are recorded in appropriate asset accounts. In contrast, revenue expenditures relate to the acquisition of benefits that do not extend beyond one accounting period; they are recorded in appropriate expense accounts for the current period.

Valuation of Fixed Assets

At date of acquisition, operational assets are recorded at cost; subsequently they are carried at cost if they have unlimited life (nondepreciable), and at cost less accumulated depreciation or depletion if they

99

Answer frame 4¹¹

1. False. Realization of carrybacks are known with certainty—if sufficient income was earned in the three preceding years. Realization of a carryforward is not known with certainty.
2. True. $2,300 = .30 \times (\$1,000 + \$2,000) + .35 \times \$4,000$.
3. False. Refund is $2,300, the total taxes paid during 19A–19C.
4. False. Net loss will be $5,300. Recall that we carry back and forward *losses,* not *taxes.* Therefore, the 19D taxable loss of $8,000 is first reduced by the $2,300 *tax savings* on the carry*back* of $7,000 of the loss to 19A–19C. At this point, Jones must estimate the tax rate that will apply to the carryforward years. In this case, the current (19D) tax rate of 40% appears to be the best possible estimate of the future years' tax rates. With $1,000 of loss carryforward, estimated to generate a tax saving at the rate of 40%, there is an additional *estimated* tax saving of $400. Therefore, the total tax saving of $2,700 ($2,300 + $400) is used to reduce the 19D net loss to $5,300 ($8,000 − $2,700).
5. True. Through 19G Jones earned $1,000 less than it lost. Therefore, we must deal with the fact that in 19H Jones Company earned the tax benefit associated with the *last* $1,000 of the 19E loss. Thus, in 19H Jones realized $450 of tax benefit (.45 × $1,000), which reduced its 19H income tax payable. The company's 19H income tax expense is $4,500 (.45 × $10,000), and its income tax payable is the remaining $4,050 [.45 × $10,000 − $1,000)].

If you missed any of the above questions, you should reread Frame 4¹¹ before proceeding.

You have now completed Chapter 11, which is the last chapter devoted to the "current" classifications. Now continue reading with Chapter 12, the first of three chapters on long-term assets.

Frame 1¹² continued

have limited life and are subject to declining economic utility to the firm. The cost of a fixed asset includes the invoice cost, *less* any cash discounts, *plus* all costs essential to get the asset "in place" and ready for the use for which it was acquired; these latter costs include such items as shipping charges, transit insurance, installation costs, repair costs, and breaking-in costs. Assets paid for with noncash considerations (stocks, bonds, other assets) must be recorded at the cash equivalent cost which is considered to be (*a*) the fair market value of the consideration given, or (*b*) the fair market value of the asset acquired, whichever is the more clearly determinable. Interest on money borrowed to purchase assets and financing charges on credit terms should not be included in asset cost. To illustrate, assume a machine is purchased at a list price of $1,000; payment is $200 cash plus a one-year note payable for the balance of $800, plus interest at 12%; the entry for the purchase would be:

Machinery	1,000	
Cash		200
Notes payable		800

In this entry the balance of $800 *was* a present value. If instead the $800 had been the total future payment (including interest), the cost of the machine would have been $914 [$200 down, *plus* the present value of $800 at 12% for one year, or $714 ($800 ÷ 1.12)]. In this case the note payable would have been recorded at its present value of $714. For a review of present value concepts see Chapter 6.

Assets Acquired by Exchange

APB Opinion No. 29, "Accounting for Nonmonetary Transactions," provides guidelines for accounting for noncash asset exchanges. The *Opinion* identifies two different types of exchanges:

a.   Exchanges involving similar assets.
b.   Exchanges involving dissimilar assets.

Exchanges of one or more *similar* assets are accounted for at the book value of the old asset. That is, the cost of the new asset is construed to be the book value of the old asset on the premise that such an exchange does not culminate an earning process.

Case A—Similar Assets.   To illustrate an exchange involving similar assets, assume that an old machine that cost $5,000 (accumulated depreciation of $1,500) is given for a new asset that has a cash price of $4,500. The entry to record this exchange would be:

Machinery (new) ($5,000 − $1,500)	3,500	
Accumulated depreciation (old machine)	1,500	
Machinery (old)		5,000

Case B—Dissimilar Assets.   Now assume that inventory that cost $4,000 (sales price of $5,000) is given for a machine that has a cash price of $4,500. This is an exchange of dissimilar assets; therefore it is construed to give rise to earnings (or loss), and fair market values are used. If we use the data given above, the entry to record the exchange would be:

Machinery	4,500	
Merchandise inventory		4,000
Gain on exchange of assets		500

Case C—Similar Assets Plus Cash Boot Paid.   Often the exchange of assets may involve the payment, or receipt, of a cash difference (often called cash boot). When the assets are *similar,* the asset received is recorded at the *book* value of the asset given up plus the cash boot paid. However, in no case should an asset be recorded at more than its current fair market value. To illustrate, assume the facts in Case A and that a $600 cash difference is paid. The entry would be:

Machinery (new)	4,100	
Accumulated depreciation (old machine)	1,500	
Machinery (old)		5,000
Cash		600

Case D—Dissimilar Assets Plus Cash Boot Paid.   Where the assets are *dissimilar* and cash boot is paid, the asset received is recorded at the *current fair market value* of the asset given up, *if known,* plus the cash difference paid. Alternatively, if that is not known, the new asset is recorded at its current fair market value. In no case should an asset be valued at more than its current fair market value. Assume the facts given in Case B and that a $600 cash difference is paid. The entry would be:

Machinery (new, not in excess of FMV)	4,500	
Loss on exchange of assets	100	
Merchandise inventory		4,000
Cash		600

Operational Asset Acquisitions and the Investment Tax Credit (ITC)

Present tax laws provide that taxpayers (corporations and others) who acquire certain long-lived assets may deduct a stipulated percentage of the cost of the asset as an investment tax credit from their income tax payable. This *credit* is not merely a deduction in arriving *at* taxes payable; it is a deduction *from* taxes payable. For example, assume in 19A that JC, Inc., paid $20,000 for a machine that was expected to remain in service for eight years. Assume further that JC, Inc.'s 19A income before tax is $37,500 and that its 19A income tax payable, prior to giving effect to the investment tax credit (ITC), is $15,000. Finally, the ITC is to be computed at 10% of the cost of qualifying asset acquisitions. In this case, JC, Inc.'s income tax payable at year-end 19A is $13,000 [$15,000 − (.10 × $20,000)].

While the income tax *payable* in this example is easy to understand, the income tax expense presents a conceptual issue: When should the ITC reduce income tax *expense* (*a*) during the year when the asset is acquired or (*b*) over the useful life of the asset? From a theoretical viewpoint the latter position is clearly the stronger. The APB took the position that the ITC should be recognized as a reduction in income tax expense over the life of the asset (called the *deferral* method). A general outcry from affected corporate taxpayers ensued, whereupon the United States Congress passed a law that enabled companies to recognize the full reduction in income tax expense in the acquisition year (called the *flow-through* method). Accordingly, at the present time, both deferral and flow-through methods are generally accepted.

To illustrate the accounting entries for the ITC, assume the data given above. Also assume that there are no other complicating income tax factors. Entries for deferral and flow-through methods are given below in parallel columns:

Deferral Method of the ITC			*Flow-through Method of the ITC*		
To record asset acquisition in 19A:					
Machinery	20,000		Machinery	20,000	
Cash		20,000	Cash		20,000
To record income taxes for 19A:					
Income tax expense . .	15,000		Income tax expense . .	13,000	
Income tax payable		13,000	Income tax payable		13,000
Deferred investment tax credit (.10 × $20,000) .		2,000			

Net income reported on 19A income statement:

$22,500 ($37,500 − $15,000)	$24,500 ($37,500 − $13,000)

Book value of machinery reported on balance sheet as of year-end 19A (straight-line depreciation for 19A is $2,500):

Cost	$20,000		$20,000
Less: Accumulated depreciation	(2,500)		(2,500)
Deferred investment tax credit	(2,000)		
Net	$15.500		$17,500

The main points of this discussion, in the context of valuation of operational assets, are that:

1. A large number of operational assets qualify for the ITC, and
2. The cost of such an asset, accounted for under the *deferral* method for the ITC, is purchase price less any deferred ITC.

Under the deferral method in 19B and subsequent years, the Deferred Investment Tax Credit will be amortized against income tax expense as follows:

Deferred investment tax credit	250	
Income tax expense ($2,000 × ⅛)		250

And, ignoring depreciation, this entry records an increase in asset book value.

Purchase of a Group of Fixed Assets

It is not unusual for a firm to purchase several assets for a lump-sum price (a basket purchase); in such cases the total price must be apportioned to the several separate assets on some logical basis such as relative market values, relative appraised values, or relative tax assessments. To illustrate, assume $90,000 was paid for a property that included a land site, a building, and some machinery; the three separate assets were appraised at: land, $10,000; building, $70,000; and machinery, $20,000. The cost apportionment and the related entry for the purchase would be:

Fixed Asset	Appraised Value	Percent of Total Cost	Apportioned Cost
Land	$ 10,000	10	$ 9,000*
Building	70,000	70	63,000
Machinery	20,000	20	18,000
Totals	$100,000	100	$90,000

* .10 × $90,000 = $9,000, and so forth.

Entry to record the purchase:

Land	9,000	
Building	63,000	
Machinery	18,000	
Cash		90,000

Indicate whether each of the following statements is true or false by writing T or F in the space provided.

_____ 1. Where assets are acquired by incurring an installment note payable, the cost of the asset is the present value of the future cash payments plus any down payment.

_____ 2. The book value of an asset that qualifies for the investment tax credit (ITC) depends in part at least on the company's method of accounting for the ITC.

_____ 3. An asset is exchanged for a *similar* asset. The *cost* of the new asset is the book value of the old asset given up.

_____ 4. Two assets are acquired with 1,000 shares of $3 par value stock that has a market value of $50,000. One of the assets is reliably appraised at $30,000 and the other asset is reliably appraised at $25,000. The assets should be recorded at $30,000 and $25,000, respectively

Check your responses with those in Answer Frame 1[12], page 104.

Frame 2[12]

Departures from Cost in Recording Fixed Assets

Fixed assets are sometimes donated to a company for certain reasons. In such cases, although there is little or no cost, the asset should be recorded at fair market value as of the date of donation. To illustrate:

1. To record the fair market value of a building ($50,000) and the land site ($5,000) donated as a plant facility:

Plant building	50,000	
Plant site—land	5,000	
Contributed capital (donated plant)		55,000

2. To record payment of transfer costs of $600 on land:

Contributed capital (donated plant)	600	
Cash		600

Answer frame 1¹²

1. True. The installment payments must be discounted to a present value—if they include interest, and the down payment is already a present value. Simply add the two present values to arrive at cost.
2. True. Other things being equal, the book value of an asset acquired by a company that flows the ITC through will be greater than the book value of an identical asset that is acquired by a company which defers the ITC.
3. True. Exchanges of *dissimilar* assets are recorded on a market-value basis. Exchanges of *similar* assets are recorded on a book-value basis (of the old asset given up).
4. True or false. The answer depends on whether the current market value of the stock given or the assets received is the more clearly determinable. If the assets received have the more clearly determinable value, they should be recorded at $30,000 and $25,000, respectively. If, on the other hand, the stock has the more clearly determinable market value, the two assets received would be recorded at $27,273 and $22,727, respectively:

   Computations:

   $$\$30,000 \div (\$30,000 + \$25,000) = .54545 \times \$50,000 = \$27,273$$
   $$\$25,000 \div (\$30,000 + \$25,000) = .45455 \times \$50,000 = \$22,727$$

If you missed any of the above, reread Frame 1¹² before beginning Frame 2¹², page 103.

Frame 2¹² continued

3. To record depreciation at end of first year (ten-year life, no residual value):

Depreciation expense	5,000	
Accumulated depreciation—plant building		5,000

In a similar manner property that has increased *substantially* as a result of the *discovery* of valuable natural resources may be restated at the higher market value. To illustrate, assume a tract of undeveloped land was acquired at a cost of $1,000 in 1950, and that in 1978 petroleum resources were discovered under it; the fair market value now is appraised at $40,000. The entries would be:

1. To record purchase value in 1950:

Land	1,000	
Cash		1,000

2. To record discovery value in 1978:

Land—appraisal increment (petroleum discovery)	39,000	
Unrealized capital increment (petroleum discovery)		39,000

3. To record depletion at end of the first year (assuming 5% of the estimated resource is removed):

Depletion expense ($39,000 × 5%)	1,950	
Land—appraisal increment (petroleum discovery)		1,950

Assets Constructed for Own Use

Companies sometimes construct certain fixed assets (such as display counters and small additions) for their own use in order to effect a cost saving, to use idle facilities, to save time, or to satisfy a need that outsiders cannot economically meet. The general rule is that all *additional* costs identifiable with the specific item should be recorded as a cost of the asset, that is, materials used, labor costs incurred, and *additional* overhead costs generated. The cost of interest on money borrowed to finance the construction should not be included as a cost but should be reported as interest expense.

Cost of Special Property

Fixed assets are recorded at cost when acquired; however, certain items of property give rise to special problems in applying the cost principle. These special problems are reviewed below.

Land.   The cost of land should be recorded in a *separate* account captioned Land or Real Estate; buildings located on the land should be recorded in a separate account since they (but not the land) are depreciable. The cost of land includes the price paid plus all incidental costs related to the transfer, such as legal fees, commissions, title fees, survey costs, and taxes due (to date of transfer) assumed by the purchaser. Costs incurred to *permanently* improve the property for the use intended, such as draining, clearing, landscaping, grading, and subdividing, are proper costs of the land. The cost of removing existing structures (less any salvage recovery) to prepare for new construction is a proper cost of the land. Costs incurred in connection with land improvements that have a limited useful life should be set up in separate accounts and depreciated.

Renovation of Old Buildings.   The capitalizable cost of an old building that is being renovated is the original purchase price and related incidentals plus the costs of renovating, repairing, and remodeling essential to make it suitable for the use intended. Building equipment, such as plumbing and electrical wiring costs, should be included in the Building account; however, removable equipment that has an essentially shorter life than the building should be set up in a separate account (e.g., Building Equipment).

Leasehold Improvements.   These are improvements placed on leased property by the lessee, such as sidewalks, buildings, and permanent equipment, that accrue to the owner of the property upon termination of the lease. The cost of such improvements should be capitalized by the lessee in a tangible fixed asset account entitled Leasehold Improvements; the cost then should be depreciated over the life of the property or the life of the lease, whichever is shorter.

Cost Outlays on Fixed Assets Subsequent to Acquisition

After a fixed asset is readied for use, it is placed in operation. Use generates numerous repairs and maintenance costs; some of these normal use costs are reviewed below. The general rule that determines whether to capitalize or to expense an outlay depends on whether the outlay creates future service potentials. If so, then capitalize the outlay; if not, then charge the outlay directly to expense.

Maintenance Costs.   Lubrication, cleaning, adjustments, and painting are classified as maintenance costs and should be recorded as expenses in the period in which they are incurred.

Ordinary Repairs.   These are routine outlays for parts, labor, and other related costs which do not add *materially* to the usefulness of the fixed asset and do not prolong its life appreciably but are necessary to keep it in normal operating condition. Ordinary repairs are *recurring* and therefore should be debited to repair expense in the period in which they are incurred.

Extraordinary Repairs.   These are *major* repairs which involve relatively large amounts, are *not recurring,* and tend to materially increase the usefulness and perhaps the remaining life of the operational asset. Accordingly, extraordinary repairs should be capitalized either by debiting the asset account or by debiting the related accumulated depreciation account, depending on whether the *usefulness* of the asset is increased or whether the *useful life* is *extended*. The effect of either treatment is to increase the *book value* of the asset; hence the depreciation rate for the remaining life of the asset must be revised.

Replacements, Renewals, Betterments, and Improvements.   These terms are used to indicate various types of *extraordinary repairs,* hence they should be accounted for as explained in the preceding paragraph. One additional problem is suggested in the case of *major* replacements; that is, the old unit removed and a new unit installed. If the original cost of the old unit can be determined, it should be removed from the accounts and the new unit recorded at its cost. To illustrate, assume the roof on the factory building is replaced at a cost of $7,000 and that the old roof originally cost $4,000; the building is 60% depreciated at the time. The related entries would be:

1. To remove the cost and depreciation on the old roof:

        Accumulated depreciation—old roof ($4,000 × 60%)   2,400
        Loss on removal of old roof   1,600
            Plant building (old roof)   4,000

2. To record cost of replacement roof:

        Plant building (new roof)   7,000
            Cash   7,000

The undepreciated balance of the cost of the building, plus the cost of the new roof, would be depreciated over the remaining life of the building.

Additions to Existing Buildings.   Frequently additions to existing buildings are constructed, in which case their cost should be capitalized in an account such as Plant Additions. The cost of the addition should be depreciated over the *shorter* period of its useful life or that of the building to which it is attached.

Retirement of Tangible Operational Assets

Operational assets may be voluntarily retired through sale, trade, or abandonment, or involuntarily through fire, storm, or similar circumstances. Irrespective of the cause, the asset should be (*a*) depreciated up to the date of the retirement and (*b*) removed from the accounts with the resultant loss or gain recognized. To illustrate, assume a machine which originally cost $60,000 is retired on July 1, 1978; accumulated depreciation at the end of 1977 was $40,000 and remaining useful life was two years at that date. Assuming the old machine was depreciated on the straight-line method and sold for $18,000, the entries would be:

1. To record depreciation for six months in 1978:

        Depreciation expense ($20,000 ÷ four semiannual periods remaining) .   5,000
            Accumulated depreciation—machine   5,000

2. To record sale of the old machine for $18,000:

        Cash   18,000
        Accumulated depreciation—machine   45,000
            Gain—disposal of fixed assets   3,000
            Machinery   60,000

True or false?

_____ 1. Interest should be capitalized as part of the cost of an asset which is constructed by a company for its own use.

_____ 2. The cost of ordinary repairs should be charged directly to expense, while the cost of extraordinary repairs should normally be capitalized.

_____ 3. The cost of donated (depreciable) assets should not be depreciated because the company did not have to expend resources to acquire the assets.

_____ 4. The cost of leasehold improvements should be charged directly to expense because the lessee does not own the principal (leased) property.

Now compare your answers with Answer Frame 2¹², page 108.

chapter 13

PROPERTY, PLANT, AND EQUIPMENT—DEPRECIATION AND DEPLETION

Frame 1[13]

Nature of Depreciation

Operational assets are acquired for use in operating a business; as they are used for the purposes for which acquired, their utility to the firm for those purposes continuously decreases. The decrease in utility is due to a combination of wear, the action of time, deterioration, inadequacy, and obsolescence. Some assets tend to decrease in utility primarily with the passage of time, others primarily through use (such as a motor vehicle). Thus, the decrease in utility of an operational asset during a given period is an expense of that period. The amount of the expense is a function of (*a*) the cost of the asset, (*b*) its estimated residual (scrap) value, and (*c*) its estimated useful life. Depreciation accounting aims to record the decrease in usefulness of the asset in a systematic and rational manner; it is a process of *cost allocation* and *not* of *asset valuation*. Depreciable assets are recorded at cost and subsequently reported on the balance sheet at cost less accumulated depreciation (i.e., book value). *Book value* of an operational asset, then, *has no necessary relationship with fair market value* at any date *except* at date of purchase.

Factors Influencing Depreciation Expense

Periodic depreciation must be computed on the basis of three factors, as follows:

1. Cost of the asset (as defined in the preceding chapter).
2. Residual value. This is the *estimated* sale value (less disposal costs) of the asset at the end of its usefulness to the company.
3. Estimated service life. This is the estimated service life to the firm expressed in terms of time (months or years) or output (units or other operating measures, such as mileage for a truck). Selection of the appropriate measure of service life depends upon the characteristics of the asset and the manner in which it is used.

Recording Depreciation

Depreciation (as computed) is debited to a depreciation expense account. There should be separate accounts for each function of the business; thus, depreciation on assets used in the sales division should be

Answer frame 2¹²

1. False. Interest should not be capitalized as part of the cost of assets. It is, by convention, construed to be the (expired) cost of borrowing cash and not part of the cost of the asset acquired with borrowed funds.
2. True. This statement reflects sound accounting reasoning.
3. False. The recorded value (in lieu of the literal cost) of donated assets should be depreciated as though the company had purchased the donated assets. The donated assets represent future service potentials; and as those service potentials expire, they should be matched against the revenue they are used to generate.
4. False. Leasehold improvements represent future service potentials; as such the cost thereof should be capitalized as an asset and depreciated in order to match revenues and expenses.

If you missed any of the above questions, you should reread Frame 2¹² before proceeding. Then continue reading with Chapter 13 on page 107.

Frame 1¹³ continued

debited to the depreciation expense account in that function whereas, if the assets were used in the factory, the debit would be to depreciation expense as an item of factory overhead. The credit for depreciation should be to an account labeled Accumulated Depreciation—(related asset identified). Depreciation usually is computed for even months; that is, transactions affecting fixed assets that occur during the first half of the month are taken into consideration during that month. Otherwise they are considered in the following month. To illustrate the recording of depreciation, assume that a fixed asset was acquired on January 1, 19A, at a cost of $11,500; it was estimated that the service life would be ten years and that the scrap value would be $2,000; however, removal and disposal costs were estimated to be $500.

Computation of depreciation for 19A (straight line):

Cost of asset		$11,500
Less: Estimated residual value	$2,000	
Removal and disposal costs	500	1.500
Cost to be depreciated over ten-year useful life		$10.000
Depreciation for 19A: $10,000 ÷ 10 years		$1.000

Entry to record depreciation for 19A, assuming the asset was utilized half of the time by the sales division and half of the time by the general administrative division:

Distribution expense—depreciation	500	
General administrative expense—depreciation	500	
Accumulated depreciation—(asset identified)		1,000

Indicate whether each of the following statements is true or false by writing *T* or *F* in the space provided.

_____ 1. Depreciation is the process of accounting for the decline in market value of an asset during the current period.

_____ 2. Assets should normally be depreciated over their economic lives rather than their physical lives.

_____ 3. The undepreciated portion of the original cost of an asset constitutes the *book value* of the asset.

Now see Answer Frame 1¹³, page 110.

Frame 2[13]

Methods of Depreciation

Under each of the *methods* of depreciation the accounting entry is the same (as illustrated above); only the *amounts* vary. That is, the several methods of depreciation deal with the problem of *computation* of the amount of depreciation for each period. Over the total life of the asset each method will "write off" the same amount of asset cost. Fundamentally, the various methods of computation of depreciation come under three broad categories: (1) those related to the passage of time, (2) those related to output, and (3) those related to the unique characteristics of the asset involved. Seven methods of depreciation in common use are reviewed below. In order to illustrate these methods in a comparative way, the following symbols and simplified amounts are used:

Item	*Symbol*	*Illustrative Amounts*
Acquisition cost	C	$ 100
Residual value	S	$ 10
Estimated service life:	n	
In years		3
In service hours (running time)		6,000
In productive output (units of output)		9,000
Depreciation rate (per year, per service hour, or per unit of productive output)	r	
Dollar amount of depreciation per accounting period . . .	D	

Straight-Line Method.   This method relates depreciation directly to the passage of time; it is simple to apply and is widely used. The formula for computing the periodic depreciation charge (annual in this case) is:

Formula

$$D = \frac{C - S}{n}$$

Illustration

$$D = \frac{\$100 - \$10}{3} = \$30 \text{ per period}$$

Alternatively, depreciation may be expressed as a *rate* (as opposed to a dollar amount). For the illustrated figures, it should be noted that the periodic (annual, in this case) rate may be expressed as either 33⅓% on net depreciable value ($90); or as 30% on cost ($100). The percent on cost generally is used; thus, annual depreciation would be $100 × 30% = $30. Frequently it is desirable to prepare a "depreciation table" to cover the life of the asset, as shown in Illustration 13–1; note that the accounting entries for each period are indicated.

The straight-line method is preferable where the following conditions are present:

1.   The decline in economic usefulness of the asset is approximately the same each period.
2.   The decline in economic usefulness of the asset is related to the passage of time rather than to use.
3.   Use of the asset is consistent from period to period.

Service-Hours Method.   This method relates depreciation to the "running time" of the asset; that is, it is related to time of productive use of the related asset. The formulas for computing the depreciation rate and the annual depreciation charge based on service hours are:

1.   To compute rate:

Formula

$$r = \frac{C - S}{n}$$

Illustration

$$r = \frac{\$100 - \$10}{6,000 \text{ hours}} = \$.015 \text{ per service hour}$$

Answer frame 1¹³

1. False. Depreciation is the process of allocating the original cost of a fixed asset, less residual value, to expense during accounting periods over which the asset is used to generate revenues.
2. True. An asset has *utility* only so long as its economic life has not expired. Many fixed assets have physical lives in excess of their economic lives.
3. True. The book value of an asset is the difference between the balance in the asset account (stated at original cost) and the associated balance in the contra asset account (accumulated depreciation).

Now turn to Frame 2¹³, page 109, and continue reading.

Frame 2¹³ continued

Illustration 13–1

Depreciation Table and Entries—Straight-Line Method (life three years)

Year	Depreciation Expense (debit)	Accumulated Depreciation (credit)	Balance Accumulated Depreciation	Undepreciated Asset Balance (book value)
0				$100
1	$30	$30	$30	70
2	30	30	60	40
3	30	30	90	10 (residual
	$90	$90		value)

2. To compute annual depreciation, assuming 3,000 service hours operated during the year:

$$D = r \times \text{service hours operated during current period}; D = \$.015 \times 3,000 = \$45$$

The service-hours method is appropriate where:

1. Obsolescence is not a primary factor.
2. The economic usefulness of the asset is directly related to working time.
3. The use of the asset can be appropriately measured (i.e., it is not applicable to an asset such as a building).

A depreciation table is shown in Illustration 13–2.

Illustration 13–2

Depreciation Table and Entries—Service-Hours Method (life 6,000 hours)

Year	Service Hours Worked*	Depreciation Expense (debit)		Accumulated Depreciation (credit)	Balance Accumulated Depreciation	Undepreciated Asset Balance (book value)
0						$100
1	3,000	(3,000 × $.015)	$45	$45	$45	55
2	2,000	(2,000 × $.015)	30	30	75	25
3	1,000	(1,000 × $.015)	15	15	90	10 (residual
	6,000		$90	$90		value)

* It is assumed that the asset was actually used in this manner and that the original estimate of useful life was confirmed.

Productive-Output Method. This method relates depreciation to the number of units of output; that is, a proportionate part (constant amount) of the total cost of the asset is apportioned directly to each unit of output. Thus, depreciation charges fluctuate directly with changes in the periodic output of the asset. The formulas for computing the unit rate and the annual depreciation charge based on units of output are:

1. To compute the rate:

    Formula   *Illustration*

$$r = \frac{C - S}{n} \qquad\qquad r = \frac{\$100 - \$10}{9{,}000 \text{ units of output}} = \$.01 \text{ per unit of output}$$

2. To compute the annual depreciation charge, assuming 4,000 units of output during the current period:

$$D = r \times \text{units of output during current period}; \quad D = \$.01 \times 4{,}000 = \$40$$

The productive-output method is appropriate where:

1. Obsolescence is not a primary factor.
2. Decrease in utility is directly related to productive use.
3. Output can be effectively measured (usually limited to one-product situations).

A depreciation table is shown in Illustration 13–3.

Illustration 13–3

Depreciation Table and Entries—Productive-Output Method (life 9,000 units)

Year	Units of Output*	Depreciation Expense (debit)		Accumulated Depreciation (credit)	Balance Accumulated Depreciation	Undepreciated Asset Balance (book value)
0						$100
1	4,000	(4,000 × $.01)	$40	$40	$40	60
2	3,000	(3,000 × $.01)	30	30	70	30
3	2,000	(2,000 × $.01)	20	20	90	10 (residual
	9,000		$90	$90		value)

* It is assumed that the asset was actually used in this manner.

Reducing-Charge Method. There are four commonly used reducing-charge (or "accelerated") methods of depreciation; they are designed to allocate the cost to depreciation in such a manner that periodic depreciation expense charges are *higher* in the early years and lower in the later years of the life of the fixed asset. These methods are based upon the theory that new assets are more efficient than old assets; therefore, the economic values of the services rendered by the asset are greater during the early life of the asset. These methods are also defended on the ground that the annual depreciation charge should decrease as the repair costs increase on the asset, thus resulting in a smooth pattern of total charges (depreciation plus repairs) to operating periods over the life of the asset. Four reducing-charge methods are reviewed in the paragraphs to follow.

Sum-of-the-Years'-Digits (SYD) Method. This method is based upon the application of a decreasing fraction each period to the cost to be depreciated. The fractions are determined by using as the denominator the sum-of-the-years' digits for the life of the asset, and as the numerator those digits in reverse order. To illustrate, utilizing the data given on page 109, the fractions by year would be computed as follows:

Denominator: Sum-of-the-years' digits: $1 + 2 + 3 = 6$.
Numerator: Digits in reverse order: 3, 2, 1.
Fractions: Period 1—3/6.
              Period 2—2/6.
              Period 3—1/6.

The depreciation amount and related entries for each year are indicated in the depreciation table in Illustration 13–4.[1]

Illustration 13–4

Depreciation Table and Entries—Sum-of-the-Years'-Digits Method (life three years)

Year	Depreciation Expense (debit)		Accumulated Depreciation (credit)	Balance Accumulated Depreciation	Undepreciated Asset Balance (book value)
0					$100
1	(3/6 × $90)	$45	$45	$45	55
2	(2/6 × $90)	30	30	75	25
3	(1/6 × $90)	15	15	90	10 (residual value)
		$90	$90		

Fixed-Percentage-on-Declining-Base Method. In applying this method the book value of the asset (undepreciated asset balance) each period is multiplied by a constant percentage rate; since a constant rate is applied to a *declining base* amount, each subsequent periodic depreciation charge will be less. The appropriate rate is computed as follows:

Formula (for the Rate)

$$r = 1 - \sqrt[n]{\frac{S}{C}}$$

Illustration*

$$r = 1 - \sqrt[3]{\frac{\$10}{\$100}} = .536, \text{ or } 53.6\%$$

* Calculation of $n\frac{S}{C}$ is readily achieved by use of logarithms or electronic calculators.

Computation of the annual depreciation charge utilizing the computed rate and the related entries are indicated in the depreciation table shown in Illustration 13–5.

Illustration 13–5

Depreciation Table and Entries—Fixed-Percentage-on-Declining-Base Method (life three years)

Year	Depreciation Expense (debit)		Accumulated Depreciation (credit)	Balance Accumulated Depreciation	Undepreciated Asset Balance (book value)
0 . .					$100.00
1 . .	(53.6% × $100)	$53.60	$53.60	$53.60	46.40
2 . .	(53.6% × $46.40)	24.87	24.87	78.47	21.53
3 . .	(53.6% × $21.53)	11.53	11.53	90.00	10.00 (residual value)
		$90.00	$90.00		

Declining-Rate-on-Cost Method. This method is based upon no particular formula; the depreciation *rate* is different for each period, being selected on an arbitrary basis. The rate selected for each succeeding period is less; hence, a decreasing depreciation charge is achieved. Application of the method is shown in the depreciation table in Illustration 13–6; observe that the second column, "Declining Rates," represents

[1] When the life of the asset is relatively long, determination of the sum of the digits is facilitated through use of the following formula:

Formula

$$SYD = n\left(\frac{n+1}{2}\right)$$

Illustration

$$SYD = 3\left(\frac{3+1}{2}\right) = 6$$

the arbitrarily selected rates for this asset. This method is unacceptable in situations where the selected rates are not logical with respect to the decrease in utility of the asset to the company.

Illustration 13–6

Depreciation Table and Entries—Declining-Rate-on-Cost Method (life three years)

Year	Declining Rates	Depreciation Expense (debit)		Accumulated Depreciation (credit)	Balance Accumulated Depreciation	Undepreciated Asset Balance (book value)
0						$100
1	55%	(55% × $100)	$55	$55	$55	45
2	25	(25% × $100)	25	25	80	20
3	10	(10% × $100)	10	10	90	10 (residual
	90%		$90	$90		value)
Scrap % .	10					
	100%					

Double-Declining-Balance Method.   Reducing-charge depreciation is acceptable for federal income tax purposes; however, the tax regulations provide that the amount of depreciation must not be more than double the amount that would result under the straight-line method when the residual (scrap) value is ignored.[2] This provision gave rise to the double-declining-balance method; under this method the fixed percentage used is simply double the straight-line rate (with residual value ignored). This rate then is multiplied each year by the *declining book value* as shown in Illustration 13–7 (rate: $33\frac{1}{3} \times 2 = 67\%$).

Illustration 13–7

Depreciation Table and Entries—Double-Declining-Balance Method (life three years)

Year	Rate	Depreciation Expense (debit)	Accumulated Depreciation (credit)	Balance Accumulated Depreciation	Undepreciated Asset Balance (book value)
0					$100
1	67%	(67% × $100) = $67	$67	$67	33
2	67%	(67% × $33) = 22	22	89	11
3	67%	(67% × $11) = 1*	1	90	10

* This represents the balance of $1 needed to leave a residual value of $10 in the asset account (cost less accumulated depreciation).

Determine whether each of the following statements is true or false.

_____ 1.   The straight-line method of depreciation is based on the assumption that the usefulness of the asset declines by a constant *amount*.

_____ 2.   For any one year the amount of accelerated depreciation will exceed the amount of straight-line depreciation.

_____ 3.   The book value of fixed assets declines more rapidly under the straight-line method than under the reducing-charge methods.

_____ 4.   When using the sum-of-the-years'-digits method of determining depreciation, a constant percentage is applied to a declining book value.

Now check your responses by comparing them with Answer Frame 2[13], page 114.

_____

[2] For tax purposes, residual value is ignored in computing depreciation. For assets acquired prior to 1954 and assets purchased secondhand (used) the maximum is one and one half times the straight-line depreciation.

Answer frame 2[13]

1. True. The straight-line method of depreciation treats depreciation expense as being incurred evenly through time.
2. False. The periodic amount of accelerated depreciation on an asset will exceed the amount of straight-line depreciation during the early years of use of the asset. The periodic amount of straight-line depreciation will be greater in the later years. But the *total* accelerated depreciation will equal the *total* straight-line depreciation.
3. False. Reducing-charge methods increase accumulated depreciation (reduce book value) more rapidly than does the straight-line method.
4. False. The statement applies to a declining-balance method such as double-declining balance, not to sum-of-the-years' digits. SYD applies a declining percentage to a constant base.

If you missed any of the above, reread Frame 2[13] before beginning Frame 3[13] below.

Frame 3[13]

Special Depreciation Systems

Special problems due to internal or external factors confronting a company may preclude use of the depreciation methods discussed above with respect to certain assets. In such cases one of several "depreciation systems" may be utilized; four systems commonly utilized are reviewed below.

Inventory System of Depreciation.   This system, also referred to as the appraisal system, bases depreciation on the results of an inventory of the asset which is taken at the end of each period. The inventory system should be used *only* where the asset is represented by a large number of small and diverse items of small unit cost, such as hand tools. In such instances, it is generally not cost efficient to depreciate each individual item. Under the inventory system, purchases of the asset are debited to the asset account in the normal manner. In comparison with the other methods, there are two differences. First, the *credit* for the periodic depreciation is entered directly in the asset account (not to an accumulated depreciation account); second, the periodic depreciation charge is the difference between the balance of the account and an inventory of the items valued at cost, adjusted down for present condition. To illustrate, assume that the Hand Tools account shows a balance of $800 and that an inventory of hand tools just taken (at the end of the accounting period) and valued at present-condition cost indicates a value of $650. The entry to record the depreciation for the period would be:

Depreciation expense—hand tools 150
Hand tools ($800 − $650)   150

Retirement and Replacement Systems.   These two systems are frequently utilized in public utilities companies in connection with such assets as line poles. The two systems are similar in that depreciation is not recorded until a unit is replaced. The basic distinction between the two systems may be summarized as follows:

1. Retirement system—the cost of the *old asset* (less its residual value) is charged to depreciation expense when it is replaced.
2. Replacement system—the cost of the *new asset* (less the residual value of the *old asset*) is charged to depreciation expense when it is replaced.

To illustrate, assume the fixed asset account Hi-Line Poles shows 100 poles in place at a cost of $100 each. Now assume five of the poles are replaced at a cost of $125 each and that the residual value of each old pole is $15. The indicated entries would be:

Retirement System:

To record retirement of the old poles:

Depreciation expense	425	
Cash (for salvage sale of old poles)	75	
Hi-Line Poles (cost of old poles)		500

To record the new poles:

Hi-Line Poles (at cost of new poles)	625	
Cash		625

Replacement System:

To record both purchase of the new and retirement of the old poles:

Depreciation expense	550	
Cash (for salvage sale of old poles)	75	
Cash		625

From the above example it is clear that the retirement system bases the depreciation charge on the older costs, whereas the replacement system bases the charge on the newer costs.

Group Depreciation.   The discussions up to this point have applied depreciation computations to each fixed asset; alternatively there are situations where groups of homogeneous assets may be depreciated as a unit. For example, the ten trucks owned by a company may be depreciated as one unit through *group depreciation procedures* which utilize an *average* depreciation rate. Under the group system, at acquisition all of the assets in the group are recorded in one fixed asset account and there is only one accumulated depreciation account. Thus, any one unit from the group cannot be considered to have a unique book value. Subsequent acquisitions are also debited to the same group asset account. *Depreciation expense* is computed by multiplying an *average depreciation rate* times the balance in the *group asset account,* irrespective of the age of the individual assets represented therein. Upon *retirement* of a unit which is a part of the group, the group asset account is credited for the original cost and the accumulated depreciation account is debited for the same amount less any salvage recovery. Therefore, the group system does not recognize any "losses or gains" on disposal of group assets. To illustrate, assume ten delivery trucks are to be depreciated as a group; the trucks cost $3,000 each and have estimated residual values of $300 and an average life of five years. The indicated entries under the group system would be:

1.   To record purchase of ten trucks at $3,000 each:

Delivery trucks	30,000	
Cash		30,000

2.   To record group depreciation at end of first year:

Depreciation expense—delivery trucks ($30,000 × 18%)	5,400	
Accumulated depreciation—delivery trucks		5,400

Computation:
Cost less residual value ($30,000 − $3,000)	$27,000	
Depreciation per year ($27,000 ÷ 5 years)	5,400	
Depreciation rate, based on asset balance ($5,400 ÷ $30,000)	18%	

3.   To record retirement of one truck (wrecked) at the end of the first year; salvage recovery $200:

Cash	200	
Accumulated depreciation (cost less residual value)	2,800	
Delivery trucks (cost)		3,000

4.   To record purchase of two new trucks (cost, $3,200 each) at start of second year:

Delivery trucks	6,400	
Cash		6,400

5.   To record depreciation at end of second year:

Depreciation expense—delivery trucks   6,012
   Accumulated depreciation—delivery trucks   6,012
Computation:
   Balance in asset account ($30,000 − $3,000 + $6,400) $33,400
   Depreciation expense ($33,400 × 18%)   6,012

Depletion

Depletion, in the accounting sense, represents the allocation of the cost of natural resources (wasting assets that are being exploited, such as gravel pits, timber stands, ore and oil deposits) to the periods in which the resource generated revenue. The concept is the same as depreciation except that the nature of the assets involved are different. That is, they have some elements of operational assets and at the same time they constitute inventory as well. To illustrate depletion, assume a gravel pit is opened on land owned and that the following data are available:

Cost of the property (net of residual value) . . . $150,000
Estimated tons that can be mined   300,000
Depletion rate ($150,000/300,000) . . . . . $.50 per ton

The entry for depletion for the first year, assuming 2,000 tons are mined and sold, is as follows:

Depletion expense (2,000 × $.50)   1,000
   Accumulated depletion—gravel pit   1,000

From the above entry, it is clear that the *productive-output* depreciation method is the most appropriate way to prorate the total cost to *units* of the natural resource that are sold.

Write-Down of Operational Assets

Operational assets should be written *down* (below cost) only when there has been an impairment of value (as operating assets to the enterprise); that is, their utility to the firm has decreased as a result of unusual circumstances that the normal depreciation did not reflect. For example, an abandoned, idle, or damaged plant (not to be repaired and reused by the firm) should be written down to its fair market value immediately after the unusual event took place; the loss on write-down should be recorded as an unusual, nonrecurring, or an extraordinary loss, depending on the circumstances that caused the loss.

Is each of the following statements true or false?

_____ 1.   The inventory depreciation system is similar in many respects to the periodic system of accounting for merchandise inventory.

_____ 2.   Retirement and replacement inventory systems cannot be successfully defended on theoretical grounds.

_____ 3.   The group depreciation method represents a departure from the cost and matching principles of accounting.

_____ 4.   Depletion expense really contains two elements: depreciation and cost of goods sold.

Now refer to Answer Frame 3[13], page 118.

chapter 14

INTANGIBLE ASSETS

Frame 1[14]

Nature of Intangible Assets

Intangible assets are those asests which benefit the enterprise through the special rights and privileges their ownership brings; they do not have the physical characteristics common to tangible assets. Examples of intangibles are: cash, prepaid insurance, short-term investments, patents, copyrights, licenses, franchises, trademarks, brand names, and goodwill. Clearly, some intangibles are current assets while others are long-term assets. This chapter deals with long-term intangible assets and with the short-term intangible prepaid insurance expense.

As with all other assets, intangibles are recorded initially at cost. Subsequent to acquisition, intangibles are accounted for and reported at cost less accumulated amortization. The APB, in *Opinion No 17,* stated that "the cost of each type of intangible asset should be amortized by systematic charges to income over the period estimated to be benefited . . . and should not be written off in the year of acquisition . . . the period of amortization should not, however, exceed forty years." Therefore, since the issuance of *Opinion No. 17* in August 1970 all long-term intangibles have been amortized, usually by the straight-line method, over their estimated "useful" lives but not to exceed 40 years. Significantly, *Opinion No. 17* also applies to any goodwill purchased as an asset. The remainder of this chapter will review the special characteristics and problems with respect to the more common intangible assets.

Patents

A patent is a right, protected by law, that enables the owner to use, manufacture, sell, and control his invention without interference and infringement by others. The legal life of a patent is 17 years; therefore, the cost of a patent should be *amortized* over the *shorter* of its remaining legal life or estimated useful life. Legal costs in defending a patent are considered a proper debit to the patent asset account. To illustrate accounting for a patent, assume X Company purchased a patent with 14 years remaining life at a cost of $17,000; subsequently $4,000 was spent for legal fees in connection with an infringement. The entries would be:

a. To record the purchase:

Patent	17,000	
Cash		17,000

b. To record cost of litigation:

Patent	4,000	
Cash		4,000

Answer frame 3¹³

1. True. In fact the two are almost identical in terms of the mechanics of computing depreciation expense and cost of goods sold. But of course the assets being inventoried are very different.
2. True. The statement is "true" if the "theoretical grounds" are those underlying the traditional accounting model, which defines depreciation as a systematic allocation of cost to periods of use. Under retirement and replacement depreciation systems, *no* depreciation is recorded if there are not retirements or replacements of operational assets. This omission violates the matching principle in those years.

    One is free, however, to posit a theory of accounting under which retirement and replacement systems are theoretically defensible. At the present time, those methods can only be defended on grounds of (*a*) expediency and (*b*) the immateriality of the difference between depreciation numbers computed under retirement and replacement systems vis-à-vis depreciation numbers computed on the basis of the methods that assign costs to periods of use.
3. False. Group depreciation simply uses groups of depreciable assets—in much the same way that dollar-value Lifo uses different inventory groups. But, like dollar-value Lifo, group depreciation is based on cost, and the periodic depreciation amounts accord with the matching principle.
4. False. Depletion expense contains only cost of goods sold. But it is computed by using a depreciation method.

If you missed any of the above questions, you should reread Frame 3¹³ before proceeding. Then continue reading with Chapter 14.

Frame 1¹⁴ continued

c. To record annual amortization:

Patent amortization expense ($21,000 ÷ 14)	1,500	
Patent (or accumulated amortization on patent)		1,500

Research and Development (R&D) Costs

In recent years, the cost of research programs has become a significant item for many companies. The accounting problems related to research costs revolve around the issue of what amounts should be expensed and what amounts should be capitalized. The nature of these problems can be appreciated when it is visualized that a research department may have hundreds of employees and that a wide variety of continuous research effort is involved, such as new product development, improvement of old products, improvement of manufacturing processes, improvement of packaging, and pure research.

While it is clear that some research and development (R&D) costs benefit future periods and hence constitute assets, FASB *Statement No. 2* (1974) requires that R&D costs be expensed as incurred. There appears to be little doubt that the FASB so ruled because of mounting criticism from within as well as from outside the accounting profession regarding the general acceptability of alternative accounting methods such as capitalization of R&D costs versus immediate expensing of R&D costs as incurred. Therefore this FASB issue was clearly not decided on the merits of theoretical arguments. Exceptions are made for (*a*) R&D costs that are incurred under contracted agreements and (*b*) R&D costs incurred by certain government-related entities. FASB *Statement No. 2* also required companies that *had* capitalized R&D costs to clear out the R&D asset accounts (as of January 1, 1975) and recognize a prior period adjustment for the write-off.

Goodwill

Goodwill represents the future potential of a business to earn *above-normal* profits; it arises from such factors as customer acceptance, efficiency of operation, reputation for dependability, quality of products, location, and financial standing. The "value" of goodwill is represented by a dollar amount assigned to the above-normal future earning capacity. *From an accounting standpoint goodwill is recognized in the accounts and reported only when actually paid for in the acquisition of a going business in an arm's-length transaction.* Thus, goodwill is recognized when a company is purchased and the total price paid exceeds the fair market value of all of the identifiable assets.

In some instances accountants are asked to assist in the estimation of a reasonable value of goodwill for negotiation purposes. The only theoretically sound approach is to calculate the *present value* of the *expected future excess earnings.* Below is a review of a number of methods.

Assume that P Company is negotiating to purchase S Company and that goodwill is a factor. After careful analysis the following estimates with respect to S Company have been derived:

Average annual earnings expected in the foreseeable future . .	$ 20,000
Estimated average future value of assets (exclusive of goodwill; liabilities are *not* assumed)	100,000

Problem: what is a reasonable value of the goodwill of S Company?

Capitalization of Earnings. Goodwill may be estimated by capitalizing the earnings at the "going" rate of return in the industry, say 12%. The computation is:

Average annual earnings expected	$20,000	
Normal rate of return for the industry	12%	
Total asset value implied ($20,000 ÷ 12%)		$166,667
Average assets expected (exclusive of goodwill)		100,000
Estimated goodwill		$ 66,667
Total Valuation Including Goodwill ($100,000 + $66,667) .		$166,667

Capitalization of Excess Earnings. The preceding computation does not consider *excess* earnings as a special factor. One way to do this is to utilize a higher rate for excess earnings, as follows:

Average annual earnings expected	$20,000	
Return on average assets expected (exclusive of goodwill) at the normal rate ($100,000 × 12%)	12.000	
Excess earnings	$ 8,000	
Goodwill: Excess earnings capitalized at 20% ($8,000 ÷ 20%)* . .		$ 40.000
Total Valuation Including Goodwill ($100,000 + $40,000) .		$140,000

* Adoption of an excess earnings capitalization rate depends on subjective factors that are unique to the purchase.

Years' Purchase of Average Excess Earnings. A more direct computation could be as follows:

Excess earnings (computed above)	$ 8,000	
Expected period of recovery of costs through excess earnings . . .	× 6 years	
Estimated goodwill	$ 48,000	
Total Valuation Including Goodwill ($100,000 + $48,000) . .	$148,000	

Present Value Computation of Excess Earnings. A conceptually sound approach to estimating goodwill is to determine the present value of future *excess* earnings purchased. To illustrate, assume for the above example that the negotiations implied the purchase of future excess earnings for ten years in addition to the identifiable assets and that the expected earnings rate was 8%. Computation of the implied goodwill would be as follows:

Average annual expected earnings purchased (estimated over ten years)	$20,000	
Average assets expected (at fair value)		$100,000
Normal annual earnings expected ($100,000 × 8%) . .	8,000	
Excess annual earnings for ten years	$12,000	
Goodwill:		
Present value of future earnings for $n = 10$, $i = 8\%$:		
$\$12,000 \times P_{\substack{n=10 \\ i=8}} = \$12,000 \times 6.7101$ (Table 6–4)		80,521
Total Valuation Including Goodwill		$180,521

True or false?

_____ 1. Intangible assets are all *long-term* intangible assets.

_____ 2. Research and development costs clearly do not benefit future periods; therefore they should be expensed as incurred.

_____ 3. Goodwill is unique among intangible assets in that it is recorded *only* when it is purchased.

_____ 4. Refer to the "Present Value Computation of Excess Earnings for Goodwill" ($80,521) in the text. Company P will record its purchase of Company S with the following entry:

Assets—listed—cash, accounts receivable, etc.	100,000	
Goodwill	80,521	
Cash		180,521

Now refer to Answer Frame 1¹⁴, page 122.

Frame 2[14]

Organization Costs

Expenditures incurred in connection with the original organization and incorporation of a corporate form of business, such as legal fees, state incorporation fees, stock certificate costs, transfer stamp taxes, underwriting costs, and, under proper circumstances, office expenses (including salaries), may be debited to an intangible asset account entitled Organization Costs. These costs may be capitalized on the theory that such costs benefit the lifetime of the entity. Since the life of a corporation frequently is indefinite, organization costs theoretically should not be amortized. However, in view of *APB Opinion No. 17,* as quoted above, the asset *must* be amortized. For practical reasons (including conservatism), organization costs frequently are amortized over an arbitrary period of five to ten years on the straight-line method.

Leaseholds

Rent paid for long periods in advance represents an asset usually referred to as a leasehold. Thus, a leasehold is a right of the lessee to use the property, and a payment made in advance for that right is an intangible asset. Leaseholds are covered in Chapter 22.

Deferred Charges

Deferred charges are expenses paid in advance, the benefit of which will extend over *several* future accounting periods. Deferred charges and prepaid expenses are identical except with respect to the number of future periods benefited (prepaid expenses are current assets). Typical deferred charges are deferred income tax debits, organization costs, rearrangement costs, and extraordinary advertising costs. Deferred charges should be reported on the balance sheet and amortized over the future periods benefited.

Life Insurance

Insurance companies sell *life insurance contracts* (policies) that, in consideration of a specified premium, call for a stipulated payment (idemnity) in case of the death of the insured. An individual can purchase a policy on his own life; likewise certain parties have an "insurable interest" in others. On this basis companies frequently purchase insurance on the lives of certain of their executives. Although there are "limited payment" policies and "term" policies, the policy commonly used for this purpose is the "ordinary life" policy, whereby premium payments are made throughout the duration of the policy. Ordinarily, a life insurance policy has a *cash surrender value* (and a loan value) starting at the end of the third policy year; this value subsequently increases each year. Obviously, then, the *net cost* of an insurance policy (i.e., the insurance expense) each year would be the difference between the premium (cash) actually paid and the increase in the cash surrender value; the latter is recorded in the accounts and reported as an intangible asset under the caption, Investments and Funds.

Casualty Insurance

Casualty insurance involves a contract whereby an insurance company, in consideration for a premium payment (paid in advance), assumes an obligation under certain circumstances to reimburse the policyholder an amount up to the *fair market value* (at date of loss) of insured property that is lost due to storm, fire, and so forth, as specified in the policy. The premium, since it is paid in advance, is debited to an asset account and then is amortized over the life of the policy. To illustrate, assume that on January 1, 19A, K Company paid a three-year premium of $6,000 for a policy on its building and the furniture therein; the indicated entries are:

a.   At date of payment:

Prepaid insurance	6,000	
Cash		6,000

b.   At end of one year (end of fiscal period):

Insurance expense ($6,000 × ⅓)	2,000	
Prepaid insurance		2,000

Prepaid insurance (like other prepaid expenses such as rent and supplies) is normally classified as a current asset on the balance sheet. Theoretically, only the prepayment that will generate benefits over one operating cycle should be classified as current, with longer term prepayments classified as deferred charges.

In order to encourage adequate insurance, policies commonly carry a *coinsurance clause* which provides that if the property is insured for less than a stated percentage (often 80%) of its fair market value at the time of the loss, the insured is a *coinsurer* with the insurance company. To illustrate, assume a property is insured for $7,000 under a policy that carries an 80% coinsurance clause; the property burns with a loss, at fair market value, of $5,600. At that date the insured property had a total fair market value of $10,000. The payment by the insurance company would be $4,900, determined as follows:

Liability of the insurance company is the lowest of the following:

1. Face of policy $7,000
2. Fair market value of the loss 5,600
3. Maximum indemnity computed by *coinsurance formula* as follows:

$$\frac{P}{.80 \times C} \times L = \frac{\$7,000}{.80 \times \$10,000} \times \$5,600 = \$4,900$$

Answer frame 1¹⁴

1. False. Some intangible assets are current items (e.g., cash, short-term investments, and prepaid insurance). The caption "Intangible Assets" on balance sheets does typically refer to long-term intangible assets, however.

2. False. R&D costs should be expensed, but not because such costs do not benefit future periods. It seems safe to hypothesize that the FASB required immediate expensing of R&D costs in order to achieve uniformity and not theoretical purity.

3. True. In general, no assets (tangible or intangible) are recorded unless they are purchased. This makes it appear that goodwill is *not unique*. However, most assets may be received (as donated capital) from donors who expect to receive nothing in return. Goodwill cannot be "donated"; therefore goodwill is unique in this respect because other intangibles (such as insurance coverage or organization costs) can be donated.

4. True. The important point is that the cost of identifiable assets should be separated from the cost of goodwill.

If you missed any of the above, reread Frame 1¹⁴ before beginning Frame 2¹⁴, page 120.

Frame 2¹⁴ continued

where P equals the face of the policy, C the fair market value of the property insured, and L the fair market value of the loss.

Accounting for a Fire Loss

When a casualty loss has occurred (due to fire, storm, earthquake, etc.), an orderly accounting procedure should be used to determine and record the amount of loss. To illustrate, assume that on July 1, 19B, the Burns Company suffered a fire loss to its building and furniture; the records were retrieved and the accounts showed the following:

	Jan. 1, 19B, Balances
Prepaid insurance (two years, 80% coinsurance clause—face: furniture, $30,000; building, $100,000)	$ 2,000
Furniture at cost (10-year life)	60,000
Accumulated depreciation (on cost)	(24,000)
Building at cost (20-year life)	200,000
Accumulated depreciation (on cost)	(60,000)

The estimated fair market value at date of fire, July 1, 19B:

	Loss	Total Value
Building	$15,000	$150,000
Furniture	10,000	45,000

The entries could be made as follows:

a. To record depreciation to date of fire (six months):

Depreciation expense	8,000	
Accumulated depreciation—furniture		3,000
Accumulated depreciation—building		5,000

b. To record insurance expired (six months), assuming the policy will continue in force:

Insurance expense 500
Prepaid insurance $\left(\$2,000 \times \dfrac{6 \text{ mos.}}{24 \text{ mos.}} \right)$ 500

c. To record fire loss:

Fire loss 7,333
Accumulated depreciation—furniture $(10/45 \times \$27,000)$ 6,000
    Furniture $(10/45 \times \$60,000)$ 13,333

Fire loss 13,500
Accumulated depreciation—building $(15/150 \times \$65,000)$ 6,500
    Building $(15/150 \times \$200,000)$ 20,000

d. To record settlement with the insurance company:

Cash $(\$8,333 + \$12,500)$ 20,833
    Fire loss   20,833
Computation:

	Furniture	Building
1. Loss	$10,000	$ 15,000
2. Face of policy	30,000	100,000
3. Formula*	8,333	12,500
Due from Insurance Company (lowest)	8,333	12,500

$\displaystyle * \text{ Furniture: } \frac{\$30,000}{.80 \times \$45,000} \times \$10,000 = \$8,333.$

$\displaystyle \text{Building: } \frac{\$100,000}{.80 \times \$150,000} \times \$15,000 = \$12,500.$

Any balance in the Fire Loss account, if it existed, would be closed to the Income Summary at the end of the period and would likely be reported as an extraordinary loss on the income statement.

Determine whether each of the following questions is true or false.

_____ 1. Attorney fees, underwriting fees, and state franchise taxes are examples of different types of organization costs.

_____ 2. In general, each dollar of premiums paid for a whole-life insurance policy contains both an expense element (for protection) and an investment element (for cash value increment).

_____ 3. Where a casualty insurance policy covers the fair market value of the assets, it is possible to actually have a *gain* associated with a casualty —inasmuch as the insurance proceeds may exceed the book value of the assets.

_____ 4. Assume that: (*a*) fair market value of insured property is $10,000; (*b*) face of insurance policy is $6,000; (*c*) fair market value of loss is $10,000; and (*d*) coinsurance provision is 80%. The insurance company will pay the insured party $6,000.

Now check your answers by referring to Answer Frame 2¹⁴, page 124.

Answer frame 2¹⁴

1. True. All the costs listed are common examples of organization costs.
2. True. This is not true in the very early years of a policy because all premiums constitute expense. But the statement is true for the general case.
3. True. This could occur, for example, if the fair market value of the insured assets exceeded their book value. Of course, this assumes that the company carried insurance in an amount sufficient to provide an indemnification in excess of book value. But it could occur; in fact it would be essentially the same as selling the assets at fair market value.
4. True. Computations:

Face of policy	$ 6,000
Fair market value of loss	10,000
Coinsurance formula amount:	
$\dfrac{\$6,000}{.80 \times \$10,000} \times \$10,000 =$	7,500
Insurance company pays lowest of the three	$ 6,000

If you missed any of the above questions, you should reread Frame 2¹⁴ before proceeding.

You have now completed Volume I of this PLAID. You should work Sample Examination 3 covering Chapters 11–14, given on page 134.

Sample examination questions

Examination 1— chapters 1–6

The reader should note that while most of the examination questions are cast in the multiple choice format, the content of the questions could be covered in a variety of different ways. That is, the questions involve (*a*) theoretical concepts, (*b*) journal entries, (*c*) computations, (*d*) short answers, and the like. Answers to the questions, along with explanations and computations, are given beginning on page 137.

1. Generally accepted accounting principles are formulated by the—
   a. Accounting Principles Board of the AICPA.
   b. Financial Accounting Standards Board of the AICPA.
   c. Securities and Exchange Commission of the U.S. Treasury Department.
   d. Representatives of various industry groups.
   e. None of the above.

2. The accrual accounting model is a reasonable alternative to—
   a. Analysis of net working capital.
   b. The fundamental accounting model, namely that Assets = Equities.
   c. Cash basis accounting.
   d. Detailed principles and procedures.
   e. None of the above.

3. Johnson Company makes all its credit sales on a 3/10, net/30 basis. For 19A, it sold 1,000 units at a sales price of $15 each, with all sales subject to the discount. The theoretically best way for Johnson to record these sales (in one entry) is:

   a.
Accounts receivable	15,000	
Sales discount	450	
Sales revenue		15,450

   b.
Sales revenue	15,000	
Accounts receivable		15,000

   c.
Accounts receivable	15,000	
Sales revenue		15,000

   d.
Accounts receivable	14,550	
Sales revenue		14,550

4. The primary theoretical consideration affecting the answer to Question 3 above involves the—
   a. Continuity assumption.
   b. Lower-of-cost-or-market rule.

    c. Consistency principle.
    d. Cost principle.
    e. Time value of money.

5. The accounts receivable accountant for Kellam Company located an error in the Kilpatrick account in the accounts receivable subsidiary ledger. In particular, a $600 sale to Kilpatrick had been posted to Kilpatrick's account as a $60 debit. This error will cause—
    a. The trial balance on the worksheet to be out of balance.
    b. An inequality between the accounts receivable control account and the total of the balances in the accounts receivable subsidiary ledger.
    c. Net income to be understated by $540.
    d. Current assets to be overstated by $540.
    e. None of the above.

6. The accumulated depreciation account is a (an)—
    a. Liability account.
    b. Equity account.
    c. Contra asset account.
    d. Expense account.
    e. None of the above.

7. The following entry

Income tax expense	65,000	
Income tax payable		35,000
Deferred income tax payable		30,000

is an example of a (an)—
    a. Regular transaction entry.
    b. Adjusting entry.
    c. Closing entry.
    d. Reversing entry.
    e. None of the above.

8. LMN Company made the following adjusting entry on December 31, 19A:

Supplies inventory	350	
Supplies expense		350

During 19A, LMN Company disbursed cash of $750 for supplies. The company had no supplies inventory at the beginning of 19A. Supplies on hand at December 31, 19A, must be:
    a. $750.
    b. $400.
    c. $450.
    d. $350.
    e. None of the above.

Questions 9–12 utilize the following data:

SA-9 has prepared the following *unadjusted* trial balance at the end of its fiscal year ended December 31, 19A:

	Debit	Credit
Cash	$ 600	
Accounts receivable	900	
Merchandise inventory	1,500	
Prepaid insurance	400	
Equipment	2,000	
Accumulated depreciation—equipment	900	
Note payable		$1,500
Accounts payable		600
Common stock		1,100
Retained earnings		900
Sales revenue		4,000
Purchases	3,100	
Rent expense	500	
Salary expense	900	
	$9,800	$8,100

At December 31, 19A, the company—

(a) Owes interest of $60 on the note.
(b) Estimates bad debt losses at $200.
(c) Owes salaries of $150.
(d) Needs to record depreciation expense of $400.
(e) Has unexpired insurance of $300.
(f) Discovers that sales revenue (as recorded in the general ledger and listed on the unadjusted trial balance) is understated by $900.
(g) Has merchandise inventory of $1,400 on hand.
(h) Is exempt from income taxation.

9. SA-9's total debits and credits, respectively, on its December 31, 19A, *unadjusted* trial balance should be—
   a. $9,800 and $9,000.
   b. $10,800 and $9,000.
   c. $9,900 and $9,900.
   d. $10,800 and $10,800.
   e. None of the above.

10. SA-9's total expenses (including cost of goods sold) for 19A are:
   a. $6,910.
   b. $6,300.
   c. $8,510.
   d. $5,510.
   e. None of the above.

11. SA-9's net income (loss) for 19A is:
   a. Net loss of $810.
   b. Net loss of $610.
   c. Net loss of $1,710.
   d. Net income of $610.
   e. None of the above.

12. SA-9's balance sheet at December 31, 19A, will report total assets of—
   a. $3,700.
   b. $3,500.
   c. $5,000.
   d. $3,900.
   e. None of the above.

13. Assume that Johnson, Inc., earned net income for 19A of $100 and that its total revenues for 19A were $900. Its closing entry for 19A could have been combined into only one entry, namely:

    a.   Income summary 900
               Revenues   900

    b.   Revenues 900
               Expenses   800
               Income summary   100

    c.   Revenues 900
               Expenses   800
               Retained earnings   100

    d.   Expenses 800
               Retained earnings 100
               Revenues   900

    e.   Expenses 800
               Revenues 100
               Retained earnings   900

14. Which of the following assumptions is absolutely necessary for asset valuation at historical cost to have meaning?
    a. Separate-entity assumption.
    b. Continuity assumption.
    c. Time-period assumption.
    d. All of the above.
    e. None of the above.

15. The statement of changes in financial position is:
    a. A supplement to the income statement.
    b. A supplement to the balance sheet.
    c. A primary financial statement.
    d. Best reported in a footnote to the financial statements.
    e. None of the above.

   For Questions 16–20 round all answers (not intermediate steps) to even dollars. Ignore income taxes on any interest.

16. Smith was to accumulate a fund of $20,000 for Toby, an industrious son, to have at his 18th birthday in order to pay for a year or two of Toby's college expenses. Smith expects to be able to earn an annual compound interest rate of 8% on the investment. How much should Smith invest today, on Toby's 15th birthday?
    a. $6,161.
    b. $1,491.
    c. $15,877.
    d. $15,770.
    e. None of the above.

17. Smith has an industrious 15-year-old daughter named J. B. Smith realizes that J. B., like Toby the industrious son, has exquisite taste in apartment furnishings, clothing, automobiles, journal paper, and the like, which means that J. B. will need quite a bit of cash while she is away at college. As a result, Smith plans to invest $20,000 today, on J. B.'s 15th birthday. Smith plans to allow J. B. to make four equal annual withdrawals from the fund created by this investment, the first of which will be available on her 18th birthday. The stated interest rate is 8% per annum, but it is compounded semiannually. In order to completely drain the fund on the date of the final withdrawal, each of J. B.'s withdrawals must be:

a. $7,075.
b. $7,043.
c. $6,972.
d. $7,089.
e. None of the above.

18. SA-8, Inc., is negotiating the purchase of a machine. The manufacturer offers the machine to SA-8 for a cash price of $35,001. SA-8, however, is only able to pay $15,000 currently, so the manufacturer agrees to let SA-8 sign a note and pay the balance, plus interest, in three monthly installments, beginning two months hence. If the interest rate on installment purchases of this type is 18% per annum and compounds annually, SA-8 would record the acquisition by making the following entry:

a.

Machine	15,000	
Cash		15,000

b.

Machine	36,801	
Prepaid interest expense		1,800
Cash		15,000
Note payable		20,001

c.

Machine	35,001	
Note payable		20,001
Cash		15,000

d.

Cash	15,000	
Note payable	20,001	
Machine		35,001

e. None of the above.

19. Refer once again to the fact situation in Question 18. Each of the installment payments will be for—
a. $3,600.
b. $6,667.
c. $6,967.
d. $5,000.
e. $11,667.

20. Each of the monthly installments referred to in Question 18 will be recorded by the *manufacturer* with an entry of the form—

a.
Note payable
Interest expense
    Cash

b.
Note payable
    Cash

c.
Interest expense
    Cash

d.
Cash
    Interest revenue

e.
Cash
    Note receivable
    Interest revenue

Sample examination questions

Examination 2— chapters 7–10

Answers are given along with explanations and computations where needed, beginning on page 140.

1. The only asset listed below for which there is no *valuation* problem is:
   a. Cash.
   b. Short-term investments in bonds.
   c. Accounts receivable.
   d. Merchandise inventory.

2. Patrick Company had poor internal control over its cash transactions. Facts about its cash position at November 30, 19A, were the following:

   The cash books showed a balance of $18,901.62, which included a November 30 deposit of $3,794.41. A credit of $100 on the bank statement did not appear on the books of the company. The balance according to the bank statement was $15,550.

   When the auditor received the bank statement on December 31, the following canceled checks were enclosed: No. 62 for $116.25, No. 183 for $150.00, No. 284 for $253.25, No. 8621 for $190.71, No. 8623 for $206.80, and No. 8632 for $145.28. The only deposit listed on the bank statement was in the amount of $3,794.41 on December 2. Check numbers reflect a chronological order of having been written.

   The cashier handles all incoming cash and makes the bank deposits personally. He also reconciles the monthly bank statement. His November 30 reconciliation is shown below:

Balance, per books, November 30, 19A		$18,901.62
Add: Outstanding checks:		
8621	$190.71	
8623	206.80	
8632	145.28	442.79
		19,344.41
Less: Undeposited receipts		3,794.41
Balance per bank, November 30, 19A .		15,550.00
Deduct: Unrecorded credit		100.00
True cash, November 30, 19A . . .		$15,450.00

   Based on the above data, it appears that the cashier has stolen—
   a. $719.50.
   b. $100.00.
   c. $619.50.
   d. $3,894.41.
   e. $519.50.

3. In general, most short-term investments in common stocks should be accounted for, under generally accepted accounting principles, at—
   a. Lower of cost or market.
   b. Cost.
   c. Market.
   d. *a* or *b* or *c,* depending on the investor company's preference.
   e. None of the above.

4. For purposes of arriving at the proper valuation of short-term investments in common stocks to be reported on the balance sheet, the appropriate unit of analysis is:
   a. Each share of common stock.
   b. Thousand-share blocks of common stock.
   c. The entire short-term portfolio of common stocks.
   d. *a* or *b* or *c,* depending on the investor company's preferences.
   e. None of the above.

Questions 5–7 are mutually independent. But they all use the following data:

Company G paid $65.50 per share for 100 shares of Jones Company stock on March 19, 19B. The next day Company G sold 50 shares of Jackson stock for $12 per share. Company G had acquired 400 shares of Jackson stock for a total outlay of $4,440 during November 19A. On December 31, 19A, the quoted price of the Jackson stock on the New York Stock Exchange was $11 per share.

During May 19B Jones Company paid a special $.50 per share cash dividend to its shareholders and in June 19B Jones also paid a 100% stock dividend (same as a 2-for-1 stock split) as well. On the date the additional (stock dividend) shares were issued, the market value of Jones stock dropped from $60 to $32 per share. But on December 31, 19B, Jones stock was quoted on the American Stock Exchange at $35 per share. On December 31, 19B, the Jackson stock was quoted at $10.00 per share.

Both investments are properly classified by Company G as *short term.*

5. On its December 31, 19A, balance sheet Company G will report—
   a. Unrealized loss on short-term investments of $40.
   b. Investment revenue of $50.
   c. Short-term investments at a book value of $4,440.
   d. Short-term investments at a book value of $4,400.
   e. Unrealized capital of $40.

6. On its income statement for the year ended December 31, 19A, Company G will report—
   a. Investment revenue of $50.
   b. Allowance to reduce short-term investments to market of $4,400.
   c. Unrealized loss on short-term investments of $40.
   d. Unrealized gain on short-term investments of $40.
   e. None of the above.

7. On its December 31, 19B, balance sheet Company G will report—
   a. Unrealized gain on short-term investments of $40.
   b. Investment revenue of $50.
   c. Short-term investments at a book value of $10,435.
   d. Short-term investments at a book value of $10,500.
   e. Unrealized capital of $65.

Questions 8 and 9 are independent of each other. But they both use the following data:

Company H made the following entry affecting its bad debt allowance as of *December 31, 19A:*

```
Bad debt expense . . . . . . . . . . . . . . . . . . . . . . .   2,000
    Allowance for bad debts . . . . . . . . . . . . . . . . . .          2,000
```

Prior to making the above entry, Company H's Allowance for Bad Debts account had a credit balance of $1,000. The amount of the entry ($2,000) was computed on the basis of an aging of accounts receivable as follows:

½% of accounts receivable of $200,000 deemed uncollectible.
1% of accounts receivable of $50,000 deemed uncollectible.
2% of accounts receivable of $10,000 deemed uncollectible.
5% of accounts receivable of $5,000 deemed uncollectible.
50% of accounts receivable of $1,000 deemed uncollectible.
100% of accounts receivable of $550 deemed uncollectible.

During *19B* Company H actually wrote off $2,800 of bad accounts as follows:

Allowance for bad debts	2,800	
Accounts receivable—Mr. A.		600
Accounts receivable—Mrs. B		200
Accounts receivable—Mr. C.		100
Accounts receivable—Mrs. D		1,900

Finally, Company H made no accounting errors in the above entries.

8. The December 31, 19A, entry given above—
    a. Had no effect on net accounts receivable.
    b. Reduced net accounts receivable by $2,000.
    c. Reduced net accounts receivable by $1,000.
    d. Reduced net accounts receivable to $264,550.
    e. Both b and d.

9. The write-off entry in 19B—
    a. Had no effect on net accounts receivable.
    b. Reduced net accounts receivable by $2,800.
    c. Reduced net accounts receivable by $1,000.
    d. Reduced net accounts receivable to $264,550.
    e. None of the above.

10. Which of the following types of costs should *not* be charged to the inventory account for a manufacturing company?
    a. Direct materials.
    b. Freight paid for shipment of direct materials to our place of business (i.e., freight-in).
    c. Direct labor.
    d. Factory overhead.
    e. All the above should be charged to inventory.

11. Inventory liquidation is a particular problem with—
    a. Fifo.
    b. Lifo.
    c. Weighted average cost.
    d. Moving average cost.
    e. Lower of cost or market.

Questions 12–18 are designed to solidify your basic understanding of a number of different inventory costing, valuation, and estimation methods. Accordingly, they all use the simplified data given below. But all the questions in this group are *independent* in the sense that no later (correct) answer depends directly on your having correctly answered an earlier question.

Superlative Examination Service (SES) writes and markets fair but reasonably rigorous academic examinations to educational institutions. On March 31, 19B, the accounting records of SES reveal the following data with respect to its inventory of examinations:

(a) Inventory on January 1, 19B – 1 examination: at Fifo cost of $2.70; at retail of $5.

(b) 19B creations (same as purchases) through March 31 – 3 examinations: at cost of $3.15 per examination; at retail of $5.40 per examination.

(c) 19B sales through March 31 – 2 examinations at $5.40 each.

(d) 19B net additional markups through March 31—$.60. These are *totals,* not per unit numbers.

(e) 19B net markdowns through March 31—$.75.

(f) 19B price indexes for inventories: January 1, 1.04; March 31, 1.08.

ROUND ALL COMPUTATIONS, INCLUDING INTERMEDIATE STEPS, TO EXACTLY (2) DECIMAL PLACES.

For the answers to Questions 12–18, select from the following:

a. $5.18.
b. $5.68.
c. $5.74.
d. $5.85.
e. $5.95.
f. $6.05.
g. $6.08.
h. $6.30.

12. SES's March 31 inventory at estimated Fifo cost, per the *retail* method, is:

13. SES's March 31 inventory at estimated average cost, per the *retail* method, is:

14. SES's March 31 inventory at the lower of estimated Fifo cost or market—*retail* method is:

15. SES's March 31 inventory at estimated dollar-value Lifo per the *retail* method is:

16. SES's March 31 inventory at (ordinary) Fifo cost is:

17. SES's March 31 inventory at (ordinary) weighted average cost is:

18. SES's March 31 inventory at (ordinary) Lifo cost is:

19. The following data relate to Construction Company, Inc.'s construction activities under one of its long-term construction contracts that was in effect during 19A and 19B.

Total costs in 19A	$100,000
12/31/19A estimate of total costs to complete the contract	500,000
Total costs incurred during 19B	300,000
12/31/19B estimate of total costs to complete the contract	300,000
Contract price	750,000

On the percentage-of-completion method, Construction Company should report for 19A and 19B, respectively, construction income of—

a. $25,000 and $50,000.
b. $25,000 and $3,571.
c. $25,000 and $28,571.
d. Cannot be determined from information given.
e. None of the above.

Sample examination questions

Examination 3— chapters 11–14

Answers are given, along with explanations and computations where needed, beginning on page 143.

1. In general, liabilities, both current and noncurrent, should be reported on the balance sheet at—
   a. Present value.
   b. Maturity value.
   c. Unamortized value.
   d. All the above, because they are the same.

2. *Contingencies* of all types (gains, losses, assets, *and* liabilities):
   a. Should never be accrued because they, by definition, have not yet materialized.
   b. Almost always involve losses.
   c. Should be accrued if it is probable that the contingency (1) has materialized and (2) can be reasonably estimated.
   d. None of the above.

3. During 19D Company R sold merchandise for $65,000, all of which was subject to warranty. Based on past experience, Company R estimates that its ultimate warranty outlay on each dollar of sales is $.02. During 19D Company R's cash outlay for warranty claims totaled $1,500. At January, 19D, Company R had outstanding warranty obligations of $1,200. Its 19D warranty expense, as reported on the income statement, is:
   a. $1,000.
   b. $1,300.
   c. $1,500.
   d. $1,200.
   e. None of the above.

4. A corporation experienced the following items pertaining to its income tax in 19E:

(a)	Statutory depletion of coal	$75,000
	Cost depletion of coal	67,500
(b)	Warranty expenses and the current year addition to estimated warranty liability	35,000
	Actual cash outlays on warranty obligations	25,000
(c)	Prior period adjustment—operating and taxable income in 19D overstated (being used to reduce current tax liability)	20,000
(d)	Realization of unused and heretofore unrecorded tax loss carryforward from 19A (when the income tax rate was 45%) (used to reduce current tax liability)	10,000

134

The tax rate of 40% applies to all items in 19D and 19E. Income before income tax on the corporation's income statement is $35,000. The only tax-related items which are treated differently for tax and book purposes are listed above.

Present the corporation's journal entry to record its income tax for 19E.

5. The cost of an operational (i.e., a fixed) asset does *not* include—
   a. Installation costs.
   b. Major renovation costs prior to bringing asset to original use.
   c. Cost of ordinary repairs that are incurred subsequent to bringing the asset to original use.
   d. Cost of repairs incurred pursuant to bringing asset to original use.

6. When a fully depreciated machine with no salvage value is retired, the entry to record the retirement—
   a. Has no effect on total assets.
   b. Reduces total assets.
   c. Increases owners' equity.
   d. Increases total assets.
   e. None of the above.

7. Corporation L paid $100,000 cash for land and a building. The estimated market values of the land and building were $25,000 and $80,000, respectively. Costs properly assignable to the land and building are, respectively:
   a. $25,130 and $74,870.
   b. $25,000 and $80,000.
   c. $20,000 and $80,000.
   d. $23,810 and $76,190.

8. Of the following statements, the false statement is:
   a. Depreciation is a process of allocating cost to periods of use of an asset.
   b. Depreciation is a process of funding the replacement of worn-out assets.
   c. Total depreciation charges over the life of an asset are the same under all depreciation methods —given one set of facts.
   d. Accelerated (reducing-charge) depreciation methods allocate relatively more cost to early years and relatively less cost to later years of use of an asset.

Question 9–11 use the following data. Questions 9–11 pertain to Methods 1–3, respectively.

Machinery that cost K Corporation $10,000 is expected to last ten years and have a $500 residual value. Several depreciation methods were applied to these data. Results are set out for Year 2 and Year 3 in the table below:

Year	Method 1	Method 2	Method 3
1	$?	$?	$?
2	1,600	1,555	950
3	1,280	1,382	950

Identify the method used and compute the first year depreciation applicable to depreciation methods 1–3. The possibilities are given below in *a–d*.
   a. Fixed-percent-on-declining balance, $2,600.
   b. Double-declining balance, $2,000.
   c. Sum-of-the-years' digits, $1,727.
   d. Straight line, $950.

9. Method 1 data pertain to which method?

10. Method 2 data pertain to which method?

11. Method 3 data pertain to which method?

12. Conceptually, goodwill is the—
    a. Present value of the expected future excess earnings.
    b. Excess of fair market value of all identifiable assets over the book value of the identifiable assets.
    c. Capitalized value of a number of future years' earnings.
    d. Present value of expected future total earnings.

13. Company Y has a fire insurance policy covering the *market value* of its merchandise inventory. The face amount of the policy is $2,500, and the policy contains an 80% coinsurance clause. On April 1 a fire destroyed three-fourths of the company's inventory that had a total fair market value of $3,900. Company Y makes its sales at a 30% markup on cost.

    As of January 1 (beginning of the company's current fiscal year) the company had the following balances in related accounts:

    Prepaid insurance (pertains to policy period that ends
        on September 30 of the current year) . . . . . $ 180
    Merchandise inventory   6,000

    Company Y made merchandise purchases of $15,000 for the current year up until the fire. Sales for the same period were $23,400. Company Y planned to use the insurance recovery to reinstate merchandise inventory that was destroyed.

    Required: Make all entries to record the insurance and the fire loss.

14. Under generally accepted accounting principles (GAAP) unidentifiable intangibles such as goodwill should—
    a. Not be amortized because they ordinarily increase in value over time.
    b. Be expensed at the time an outlay for an intangible is made.
    c. Be amortized over a period not exceeding 40 years.
    d. Be amortized over a period of ten years.
    e. None of the above.

15. Under GAAP research and development (R&D) costs should ordinarily—
    a. Be amortized on the same basis as any other intangible.
    b. Be capitalized and *not* amortized because such costs are expected to benefit future periods over an indefinite future period of time.
    c. Be expensed at the time R&D outlays are made.
    d. Be capitalized and amortized over a relatively short period of time.
    e. None of the above.

Answers to sample examination questions

Examination 1—chapters 1–6

1. *e.* Explanation: The answer would have been *b*, the Financial Accounting Standards Board if the phrase "of the AICPA" had not been included—because the FASB is autonomous and therefore is not a part of the AICPA.

2. *c.*

3. *d.* Explanation: This answer records the asset, Accounts Receivable, and the related revenue, Sales, at present value, that is, net of any sales discount that represents interest.

4. *e.* Explanation: This answer follows directly from the explanation of the answer to Question 3.

5. *b.*

6. *c.*

7. *b.*

8. *d.* Explanation: Supplies on hand at December 31, 19A, must be $350. The adjusting entry given records an increase in the asset, Supplies Inventory. This implies that when the company disbursed $750 cash for supplies, they debited the expense account, Supplies Expense. Therefore, the year-end adjustment must record the asset (Supplies Inventory) that is on hand at year-end, $350. This year-end adjustment also accomplishes the dual objective of reducing *recorded* Supplies Expense to the correct balance of $400 ($750 debit—$350 credit).

9. *c.* Explanation: Three errors in the unadjusted trial balance must be corrected. *First*, the $900 balance in the Accumulated Depreciation account should be listed as a credit, not a debit. *Second*, the debit column is mis-added. The total debits (excluding accumulated depreciation) should be $9,900. *Third*, Sales Revenue is understated by $900 (as given in item (*f*)). The total credits (including accumulated depreciation of $900 and Sales Revenue of $4,900) are also $9,900.

10. *d.* Explanation: Expenses listed on the unadjusted trial balance are:

a.	Beginning inventory of $1,500	$1,500
b.	Purchases of $3,100	3,100
c.	Rent expense of $500	500
d.	Salary expense of $900	900

To the above expenses must be added (subtracted):

a.	Interest expense of $60	60
b.	Bad debt expense of $200	200
c.	Accrued salary expense of $150	150
d.	Depreciation expense of $400	400
e.	Insurance expense of $100	100
f.	Ending inventory of $1,400 must be subtracted	(1,400)
		$5,510

11. **b.** Explanation: Total revenue ($4,900) minus total expense ($5,510) equals net loss of $610.

12. **a.** Explanation: Total assets of SA-9's 12/31/19A balance sheet are comprised of:

a.	Cash	$ 600
b.	Accounts receivable, net of $200 Allowance for Doubtful	
	Accounts	700
c.	Merchandise inventory	1,400
d.	Prepaid insurance	300
e.	Equipment, net of $1,300 accumulated depreciation . .	700
		$3.700

13. **c.** Explanation: Answer *c* is better than Answer *b* because the credit to Income Summary in Answer *b* must later be closed to Retained Earnings. Therefore, *c* is the best answer.

14. **b.** Explanation: The separate-entity assumption and the time-period assumption are both necessary—but for reasons that are not necessarily related to valuation of assets at historical cost. The continuity assumption is absolutely necessary for asset valuation at historical cost to have meaning because in the absence of this assumption, liquidation is implied, and assets are valued at net realizable value (selling price less costs of disposal) when liquidation is imminent.

15. **c.**

16. **c.** Explanation: This problem can be solved as a future amount of 1 problem or as a present value of 1 problem. Recall that PV of 1 is the reciprocal of FA of 1. The solution proceeds as follows:

Toby's Birthdays

Step 1—

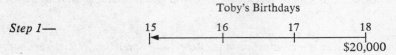

*Step 2—*PV of $20,000 at 8% for 3 periods
 = $20,000 × PV of 1 at 8% for 3 periods

*Step 3—*PV of $20,000 at 8% for 3 periods
 = $20,000 × .79383 (from Table 6–2)
 = $15,877

17. **d.** Explanation: This problem involves the present value of a deferred annuity. Furthermore, the effective interest rate is greater than the stated interest rate of 8% because interest is compounded semiannually.

Therefore, the effective interest rate of 8.16% $\left[\left(1 + \dfrac{.08}{2}\right)^2 - 1\right]$ must be used as *i* in the problem.

The solution proceeds as follows:

J.B.'s Birthdays

Step 1—

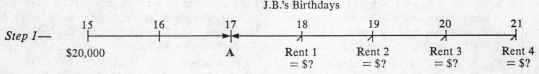

Thus, the dollar amount at point **A** equals both (1) the FA of $20,000 at 8.16% for 2 periods *and* (2) the PV of an annuity of 4 rents of $? each at 8.16%. Therefore, the solution will involve two equations, and the table values will *not* be useful since they do not include future amounts or present values computed using an interest rate of 8.16%. As a result we must use the formulas for FA and PV.

*Step 2—*Eq. 1: **A** = FA of $20,000 at 8.16% for 2 periods
  Eq. 2: **A** = PV of 4 rents of $? each at 8.16%
*Step 3—*Eq. 1: **A**= $20,000 × (1.0816)²
    = $20,000 × 1.16986
    = $23,397

Now we substitute $23,397 (the value of **A**) into Equation 2, and solve for the dollar value of each rent. Let *R* represent the dollar value of each rent.

$$\text{Eq 2: } \$23,397 = R \times \frac{1 - \dfrac{1}{(1.0816)^4}}{.0816}$$
$$= R \times 3.30037$$
$$R = \$23,397 \div 3.30037$$
$$= \$7,089$$

18. *c.*

19. *c.* Explanation: The principal debt of $20,001 is divided into three monthly payments of $6,667 each. To this must be added one third of the total interest of $900, computed as follows:

Interest expense for first two months . . .	$ 600	($20,001 × .015 × 2)
Interest expense for third month	200	[($20,001 − $6,667) × .015]
Interest expense for fourth month	100	[($20,001 − $6,667 − $6,667) × .015]
Total interest	900	
Divided into three equal parts . . .	÷ 3	
Interest added to each monthly payment of principal	300	
Monthly principal payment	6,667	
Total monthly payment	$6,967	

There are two subtleties in this problem:
a. The cash price of the machine ($35,001) does *not* include interest.
b. The interest compounds annually; therefore, for interim periods (such as months or quarters) within a year, the interest is simple, not compound.

20. *e.*

Answers to sample examination questions

Examination 2—
chapters 7–10

1. *a.*

2. *a.* Explanation: One fruitful way to approach this problem is to prepare a correct reconciliation of bank to book balances, then to compare the book balance per this correct reconciliation to the book balance (of $18,901.62) per the incorrect reconciliation given. The difference represents the suspected theft. The correct reconciliation appears below (in the typical format):

Balance per bank, 11/30/19A	. . . .			$15,550.00
Add: Deposit in transit .	. . . .			3,794.41
Deduct: Unrecorded credit	. . . .			(100.00)
Outstanding checks:				

Number	Amount	
62	$116.25	
183	150.00	
284	253.25	
8621	190.71	
8623	206.80	
8632	145.28	(1,062.29)

Balance per books, 11/30/19A, per correct reconciliation	. .	18,182.12
Balance per books, 11/30/19A, per incorrect reconciliation	. .	18,901.62
Apparent amount of cashier theft		$ 719.50

3. *a.*

4. *c.*

5. *d.* Explanation: 400 shares of Jackson common at $11 per share = $4,400. This market value is less than cost of $4,440.

6. *c.* Explanation: Cost ($4,440) minus LCM ($4,400) = Unrealized *loss* of $40—to be reported on the income statement.

7. *c.* Explanation: LCM for the entire portfolio (of two stocks) is:

		Total	
Stock	No. Shares at 12/31/19B	Cost	Market
Jackson	350	$ 3,885	$ 3,500
Jones	200	6,550	7,000
	Total . . .	$10,435	$10,500
	LCM . . .	$10,435	

8. *b.*

9. *a.*

10. *e.*

11. *b.*

12. *f.* Computations:

	Cost	Retail	Cost Ratio
Beginning inventory	$ 2.70	$ 5.00	
Purchases	9.45	16.20	
Net additional markups		.60	
Net markdowns		(.75)	
Cost ratio determination	9.45 ÷	16.05	= .59
Goods available for sale, at retail		21.05	
Sales, at retail		(10.80)	
Ending inventory, at retail		10.25	
Times cost ratio		× .59	
Ending inventory, at estimated cost	$ 6.05		

13. *e.* Computations:

	Cost	Retail	Cost Ratio
Beginning inventory	$ 2.70	$ 5.00	
Purchases	9.45	16.20	
Net additional markups		.60	
Net markdowns		(.75)	
Goods available for sale—cost ratio determination . . .	12.15 ÷	21.05	= .58
Sales, at retail		(10.80)	
Ending inventory, at retail		10.25	
Times cost ratio		× .58	
Ending inventory, at estimated cost	$ 5.95		

14. *c.* Computations:

	Cost	Retail	Cost Ratio
Beginning inventory	$ 2.70	$ 5.00	
Purchases	9.45	16.20	
Net additional markups		.60	
Cost ratio determination	9.45 ÷	16.80	= .56
Net markdowns		(.75)	
Goods available for sale, at retail		21.05	
Sales, at retail		(10.80)	
Ending inventory, at retail		10.25	
Times cost ratio		× .56	
Ending inventory, at estimated cost	$ 5.74		

15. *b.* Computations:

	Cost	Retail	Cost Ratio
Beginning inventory	$ 2.70	$ 5.00	
Purchases	9.45	16.20	
Net additional markups.		.60	
Net markdowns		(.75)	
Cost ratio determination	9.45 ÷	16.05 =	.59
Goods available for sale, at retail		21.05	
Sales, at retail		(10.80)	
Ending inventory, at retail		10.25	
Index (1.08/1.04)		÷ 1.04	
Ending inventory, at retail deflated to base year retail prices		9.86	
Comprised of:			
Base year layer carried over from 19A	2.70	5.00	
Added layer—during 19B, at retail deflated to base year retail prices		4.86	
Times index		× 1.04	
Added layer—19B, at current year retail prices		5.05	
Times cost ratio		× .59	
Added layer, at estimated cost	2.98		
Ending inventory, at estimated cost	$ 5.68		

16. *h.*
17. *g.* Computations:

	No. Units	Unit Cost	Total Cost
Beginning inventory	1	$2.70	$ 2.70
Purchases	3	3.15	9.45
	4		$12.15
Weighted average cost ($12.15 ÷ 4)		$3.04	
No. units in ending inventory		× 2	
Total cost			$ 6.08

18. *d.*
19. *b.* Computations:

19A $\dfrac{\$100,000}{\$100,000 + \$500,000} \times (\$750,000 - \$600,000) = \$25,000$

19B $\left[\dfrac{\$100,000 + \$300,000}{\$100,000 + \$300,000 + \$300,000} \times (\$750,000 - \$700,000) \right] - \$25,000 = \$3,571$

Answers to sample examination questions

Examination 3—
chapters 11–14

1. *a.*
2. *d.* Explanation: Answer *a* is false because contingent losses should be accrued under appropriate circumstances. Answer *b* is false because contingent gains and assets do not involve losses. Answer *c* is false because contingent gains and assets should not be accrued. Therefore, the answer is not *a* or *b* or *c*. It is *d,* none of the above.
3. *b.* Computation: $65,000 × .02 = $1,300.
4. Entry is:

Income tax expense (per schedule)	11,000	
Deferred income taxes [.40 × ($35,000 − $25,000)]	4,000	
Income tax payable (per schedule)		3,000
Extraordinary gain—realization of tax loss carryforward		
(.40 × $10,000)		4,000
Prior period adjustment (.40 × $20,000)		8,000

Computations:

Item	Income Tax Expense	Income Tax Payable
Income before tax	$ 35,000	$ 35,000
Add back cost depletion ⎱ a permanent difference	67,500	67,500
Deduct statutory depletion ⎰	(75,000)	(75,000)
Add back warranty expense ⎱ a timing difference		35,000
Deduct warranty outlays ⎰		(25,000)
Deduct prior period adjustment		(20,000)
Deduct tax loss carryforward		(10,000)
Base for computing tax	27,500	7,500
Income tax rate	× .40	× .40
Income tax	$ 11,000	$ 3,000

5. *c.*
6. *a.*
7. *d.* Computations:

Land $\dfrac{\$25,000}{\$25,000 + \$80,000} \times \$100,000 \quad = \$\ 23,810$

Building $\dfrac{\$80,000}{\$25,000 + \$80,000} \times \$100,000 \quad = \underline{\ \ 76,190}$

$$\underline{\underline{\$100,000}}$$

8. *b.*

9. *b.* Computations: Year 1—$10,000 × .20 = $2,000; Year 2—$8,000 × .20 = $1,600.
10. *c.* Computations: Year 1—$9,500 × 10/55 = $1,727; Year 2—$9,500 × 9/55 = $1,555.
11. *d.* Computations: Year 1—$9,500 × 1/10 = $950; Year 2—same as for Year 1.
12. *a.*
13. To close beginning inventory:

Income summary	6,000	
Merchandise inventory		6,000

To set up ending (April 1) inventory:

Merchandise inventory	3,000	
Income summary		3,000

Computation by gross profit estimation method (see Chapter 10):

Beginning inventory	$ 6,000
Purchases	15,000
Goods available for sale, at cost	21,000
Cost of goods sold ($23,400 ÷ 1.30)	18,000
Estimated *cost* of inventory destroyed	$ 3,000

To record fire loss:

Fire loss (¾ × $3,000)	2,250	
Merchandise inventory		2,250

To record insurancy recovery:

Cash	2,344	
Fire loss		2,250
Gain on disposal of inventory		94

Possible amounts of recovery (lowest of the following):

Face amount of policy	$2,500
Market value of loss (¾ × $3,900)	2,925
Coinsurance formula:	
$\frac{\$2,500}{.80 \times \$3,900} \times \$2,925$	2,344

To record expiration of prepaid insurance up to date of loss:

Insurance expense (⅓ × $180)	60	
Prepaid insurance		60

14. *c.*
15. *c.*

INDEX

A

Accounting
  definition, 1
  model, 10–11
  policies, 94*
  principles, 6–8
  process, 11–15
  theory, 4–9
Accounting changes, 23, 56–57*
  estimate, 58–59
  principles, 57–58*
  reporting entity, 57*
Accounting errors, 59*, 61*
Accounts receivable, 51
Accrued liabilities, 87
Adjusting entries, 13
Allocation of income taxes
  interperiod, 90–94
  intraperiod, 94
Amortization of bond premium and
  discount; *see* Bonds, amortization
  of premium and discount
Amortization of intangible assets; *see*
  Intangible assets, amortization
Amount of annuity; *see* Future
  amount of annuity
Amount of 1; *see* Future amount of 1
Annuity
  future amount, 35
  present value, 37
Annuity due, 39
Appropriations of retained earnings,
  18–19*
Assets, definition of
  current, 25
  fixed, 26
  operational, 26
  other, 26

B

Bad debts, 52
Balance sheet
  composition of, 25
  example, 26, 95*
  importance, 27–28
  from incomplete data, 61–62*

Bank reconciliation, 47
Bonds
  amortization of premium and dis-
    count, 48–49*, 51–52*
  convertible, 53*
  early extinguishment, 54*
  investments in, 47–50*
  nature of, 46*
  payable, 51–55*
  refunding; *see* Bonds, early extin-
    guishment
  reporting, 53*
  serial, 54*
  valuation, 47*

C

Capital
  changes after formation, 24–32*
  general, 2*
  illustrated on balance sheet, 26
  reporting example, 3*
Capital expenditures, 99
Capital stock, 27
Cash, 45
Cash dividends, 15*
Closing entries, 14–15
Common stock; *see* Corporations,
  stock
Comparative financial statements, 95*
Contingent liabilities, 89
Contributed capital in excess of par,
  27
Corporations
  capital, 1–8*, 10*
  stock, 4–5*
  types of, 1*
Cost
  definition, 18
  principle, 6
Current assets, 25
Current liabilities, 26, 85
Current replacement cost accounting,
  111–15*
  financial statements, 115*
  holding activities, 111*
  operating activities, 111*

D

Deferred charges, 26
Deferred income taxes; *see* Income
  taxes, allocation for timing differences
Depletion, 116
Depreciation
  declining-rate-on-cost method, 112–
    13
  double-declining-balance method,
    113
  fixed-percentage-on-declining-bal-
    ance method, 112
  group system, 115
  nature of, 107
  productive-output method, 111, 116
  retirement and replacement systems,
    114–15
  service-hours method, 109
  straight-line method, 109
  sum-of-years'-digits method, 111
Discounting notes receivable, 54–55
Dividend, 5–6*
  cash, 15*
  liability, 15*
  liquidating, 15*
  property, 15*
  to recipient, 44*
  revenue, 44*
  stock, 16–17*
Dollar-value Lifo, 72–75

E

Earnings per share, 33–35*
Error corrections, 59*
Estimated liabilities, 88
Expense, definition, 18
Extraordinary items, 23

F

Fifo, 68–69
Financing leases, 87–89*
Fire loss, 122
Fixed assets; *see* Operational assets
Footnotes, 21, 29

---

* Volume 2.

* Volume 2.